The Wand of Merlin

by

Ronan Coghlan

BANGOR:

XIPHOS BOOKS, 2017

Publisher:

Xiphos Books,
1, Hillside Gardens,
Bangor,
BT19 6SJ,
Northern Ireland.

ISBN: 978 09935261-1-4

Chapter One

Gavin opened one eye, decided the early morning air was not good for it and closed it again. Then suddenly both eyelids shot up. Today was the first day of the summer holidays. The grim buildings of Richill School no longer stood waiting for his arrival. His ferocious form master, Mr Cadogan, a man who looked like Billy Connolly with additional hair, would not feature in his life today. The stern headmaster, who bore the rather intimidating name of Dr Cudgell, would not gaze scornfully at his youthful charges. Gavin was free!

Gavin had also his thirteenth birthday to look forward to. He had dropped hints about what presents would suit him left, right and centre in a way that could hardly be characterised as subtle.

At that moment his younger brother Thomas (aged 8, but with a mind far in advance of that) looked into his room. Thomas had a head that seemed somehow too big for the rest of him. He was also full of craft and guile. Had he been nasty as well, he could have wrought untold havoc, but happily he was a cheerful, good-natured soul.

"Brother mine," he intoned, "your breakfast lies waiting on the table. Your bowl of cereal is crackling, ready to be eaten, your toast longs for your jaws to champ upon it. Get that lazy carcass from your bed and hurry downstairs or you will feel the wrath of Mother which is nothing to be scoffed at. She shows signs of impatience already."

That reminded Gavin he must tell Thomas about the Wilkins Mystery. Sure enough, Thomas was young, but Thomas's brain would be a useful aid to any investigation. Certainly, it was odd.

Gavin pulled himself from his bed, dressed slowly as sleepiness still clung to him somewhat and ambled down the stairs. His Mother, who did not suffer latecomers gladly, was scuttling around the kitchen and grousing. Gavin paid scant attention to this, as his Mother always seemed to have something to grumble about and the something usually had to do with him. Thomas never got grumbled at, as he had learned a thousand sneaky ways to avoid the arrows of his Mother's wrath.

I will mention Father in passing, as he was the type of person who was usually mentioned in passing, as there was never a great deal to say about him. Father disliked fuss. He liked to keep out of the limelight. He enjoyed getting on with life peacefully. At his desk in Egality Finance, where he followed some kind of career which involved dealing with money, he pursued his work in silent manner, rarely raising his head from his computer. Some of his colleagues didn't even know his name. At breakfast he was generally shielded by his newspaper, *The Daily Reporter*. An occasional grunt requesting the butter or other appropriate condiment was all you ever heard from him.

Needless to say, this made Mother, who was busy and active, irritable at times, but on the whole it suited her, as Father never uttered any idea or opinion which conflicted with hers. The reason they had such a successful marriage was because he was a silent partner.

"I have to go out today," announced Mother.

Mother worked from home for some magazine for which she wrote a large number of articles which were generally about celebrities whom she had never met, never seen but about whom she had a great deal to say. However, today she had to interview an actual famous poet, one Samson Strange, and she was meeting him and a photographer at the Bloomington Hotel - referred to by the locals as the Bloomin' Hotel - in Monster Street. Monster Street, I hasten to add, did not contain monsters. It had originally been called Minster Street at some long ago date, but somehow the name had become corrupted. Gavin always felt it should at least contain a ravaging dinosaur, but it didn't. It was an ordinary, run-of-the-mill street, served by a No 7 bus.

"You and Thomas are to behave," Mother added in what the children regarded as her firm tone. "I don't want to come home and find the place in a shambles. There's my taxi now."

"Uh!" said Father in acknowledgement.

Although the taxi waited without, it took Mother almost five minutes to gather her paraphernalia together, extract a promise from her children that they would do the dishes, make sure everything that ought to be turned off was turned off (Father couldn't be depended on for this) and finally hit the trail.

As Father continued to read his newspaper, Gavin and Thomas had a rice krispie flicking session across the table and then, when Gavin had finished his breakfast, they went upstairs. Father rose and made his way out to his car, a vehicle of nondescript colour which lay in the driveway. He was a contented man in his own little world.

Upstairs, Gavin spoke to Thomas and there was a certain seriousness in his voice.

"Thomas, I need to ask for the use of your brain."

"My brain is of a large quantity," said Thomas. "Are you sure you want to use it all?"

"Yes," Gavin replied. "Look at this."

He went to a shelf in his room and took down what a large scrapbook, bound in leather.

"That's one of the Form Yearbooks from the school library," observed Thomas. "We're not supposed to take them out. Even if we did, they're dead boring anyway. There's nothing in them but photographs of the class going back year after year until about Shakespeare's time."

"There's something unusual about this one," informed Gavin rather grimly. He opened the volume which had the Class Number, 8-1 emblazoned on its cover.

"This better be interesting," muttered Thomas. "I can't be bothered looking at your mugshot."

Gavin opened the book at the last photograph, which had been taken shortly before the end of term. Thomas looked at it closely.

"Oh, there's you," he exclaimed. "You look a right prune."

"Never mind me and my prunishness," retorted Gavin, a touch of sharpness in his voice. "Who's that?"

He pointed to a rather fat boy standing in about the centre of the lined-up classmates. The boy had a big grin on his face.

"That's that podgy fellow, Gustavus Wilkins," replied Thomas airily. "You can't mistake him."

"Right," confirmed Gavin. "Now look at last year's class. Who's that?"

"It's Gustavus Wilkins again," said Thomas, a curious tone in his voice. "But hang on a minute. He couldn't have been in 8-1 last year. He'd have gone on to 9-1 this year. Besides, he's a new boy - I remember he only joined the school last September in time for this year."

"You're getting there," said Gavin. "Now, look at the photograph of the year before last. Whose face is that?"

"Gustavus Wilkins again," said Thomas slowly. "And he looks the same age in all the photographs. About 12 - the right age for 8-1. And look - he's in the previous one too."

They continued to look through the photographs until they reached 1967, which was the year in which these photographic records commenced. Gustavus Wilkins was in all of them - never changing age, always grinning cheekily.

"Could he have done it with computers for a joke?" Thomas suggested.

"Maybe he could," Gavin agreed, "but that would require an awful lot of time and effort. I don't see why he would. Not for a joke that nobody might ever notice. I don't know that he *could*."

"Well, there's only one way to find the explanation for this," decided Thomas. "Go to the Wilkins abode. Confront him. Demand replies."

"I'm ahead of you there," his big brother informed him loftily. "I got his address from Johnny Mudd. It's an easy one to remember. 21, Tandem Road."

"Funny name for a road," said Thomas. "Maybe it was called after someone's favourite bicycle. Anyway, speaking of bicycles, you've got one, so cycle over there and wring the truth from him."

Gavin looked up Tandem Road on a well-known search engine that rhymes with boogle. It was there all right, however oddly it had been named.

"Take your key," advised Thomas. "I might be out when you get back."

Gavin quitted the house. As he did so, the man next door came into his garden. He was called Mr Blackman. He didn't get on very well with Gavin, for some years ago Gavin had had a rabbit which could escape from any hutch and Mr Blackman had been growing carrots for some kind of show. The carrots had disappeared and Mr Blackman had harboured deep suspicions of the rabbit, but he had never been able to prove anything. Then the rabbit (Bun by name) had escaped once more, entered Mr Blackman's garden and bitten off the end of his cat's tail. This was too much for Mr Blackman. With baseball bat in hand, he had entered his neighbours' garden, intent on the destruction of Bun. Bun had charged him, avoiding the bat and biting Mr Blackman on the ankle. He had then rushed through an open gate and headed for the wilderness, where perchance he wanders yet.

Mr Blackman gave Gavin a scowl. After two years, the episode with Bun still rankled. Gavin ignored him. Next door, apparently digging up some weeds, was Caroline Zuppinger.

"Hi, Jug Ears," she greeted Gavin.

She and Gavin were not enemies. They just had developed the habit of calling out insults to each other whenever they met. Caroline was an American whose father worked for one of those multinational companies trying so hard to pollute the planet. She was slightly taller than Gavin or so it seemed, as her swathe of chestnut locks added to her height.

"Morning, Cow Face," called Gavin affably.

He mounted his bicycle and pedalled off. Thomas entered the garden.

"Where's your brother off to?" wondered Caroline.

Thomas, who always liked a good gabble, told her.

Meanwhile, Gavin was bicycling up a steep hill called The Gripe. It had been called this since before the area had been built up. Somehow, the name had remained. Other streets round about bore such unlikely names as Tennessee Gardens (none of the occupants had ever seen Tennessee), Oldcastle Street (which had never boasted any kind of castle), Bulstrode Crescent (named after Bulstrode, whoever he was - an admiral, I think) and Bismarck Road (no, I don't know how it came to be called that either). Then at last he reached Tandem Road.

Tandem Road was a perfectly ordinary looking cul-de-sac. No air of mystery hung about it. Gustavus Wilkins' house was at the further end. It looked perfectly normal too. That is to say, it had a door, windows, a garden, a garden path and a garden gate. Gavin went up the aforementioned garden path and knocked on the door.

Chapter Two

The woman who answered the door was pale. Not pale like a vampire, more kind of colourless. Her head was capped with fair hair that looked wishy-washy, as though she had started to dye it and then given up. Her eyes had a certain quality of blankness that made Gavin wonder if she had visual difficulties.

"Yes?" she said in a toneless voice.

"I've - er - I've come to see Gustavus," said Gavin a little uneasily. While the woman didn't look in the least threatening, she didn't look *right*.

The woman, whom Gavin assumed to be Gustavus' mother, gestured vaguely towards a door at the far end of the hallway.

"There," she said.

Gavin walked down the hall. The woman made no attempt to follow him. After a couple of minutes, he heard the hall door closing. He looked behind him and saw the woman wasn't there. She must have slipped into a side door leading off the hall.

Like most schoolboys, Gavin didn't pay much attention to the décor of the hall. The kind of wallpaper held scant interest for him. Ditto, the picture of a Mexican bush. The carpet looked normal as carpets go. He approached the door behind which Gustavus was apparently to be found.

This door seemed suddenly slightly menacing to Gavin, in a way the front door had not. It was stained a rich brown and this made it seem perhaps solider than it was. Beneath one arm he clutched the Form Year Book. For the first time, he began to wonder how he would ask Gavin about the enigma of his multiple appearances. Supposing there was some dreadful reason for them? He wasn't sure what dreadful reason there could be, but for some reason the uncanny quality of Gustavus Wilkins' being in every picture every year struck him more forcefully than it had before.

He wondered if he should knock. He decided this would not be necessary as the woman, in indicating the door, had more or less given him permission to enter it. He opened it, perhaps a little more slowly than he was accustomed to opening doors. Inside was Gustavus Wilkins.

The room was rather strangely furnished. It had a long table stretching across it, virtually cutting it in two. On the table were all manner of strange looking instruments and objects which Gavin was unable to name. One of them was a little box on wheels which was actually moving about, propelled by steam coming out of a small pipe at the back, but which never seemed to bump into any of the other strange thingamagigs. The room was shelved all around with books, some of them looking old enough to have been read by Noah in the ark, vessels that looked as though they belonged in a laboratory and a number of potted plants. The alarming thing, however, was that Gustavus was holding what looked like a plastic gun and pointing it at him.

Well, no. On closer inspection Gavin saw it really looked more like a water-pistol. It was coloured a bright blue and, although it had a trigger, funnily enough it didn't seem to have a trigger guard.

"In the name of Methuselah's grandfather, Wilkins, why are you pointing that thing at me?" Gavin demanded.

I should tell you that most people addressed Gustavus as Wilkins, finding Gustavus something of a mouthful and discovering he did not care for Gus. His teacher, Mr Cadogan (the Billy Connolly lookalike) had once asked him where he got his name. Gustavus told him it was an old family name, taken from an ancestor who had been burned at the stake for having eaten his children. Mr Cadogan had asked no more.

"This," said Gustavus, "is a deadly instrument."

"That," said Gavin, "is a pathetic looking water-pistol."

"Oh, is it?" Gustavus replied, a touch of rancour in his voice. "Take a look at that pot."

The pot in question was on one of the shelves. It was no great monument to the potter's art. It looked as if it might have been made in a pottery class by a beginner, which was in fact the case. Gustavus pointed his instrument at it and pulled the trigger.

A jet of white light shot from the "water pistol" and struck the pot, smashing it into smithereens. Gavin's jaw dropped.

"What in the name of sanity did you have in that?" he demanded.

"Dead cool," said a voice from the open window behind Gustavus.

Both looked in that direction. Gazing through it was a large head with spectacles. If you haven't guessed already, it was Thomas. He proceeded to clamber through the (open) window.

"Thomas, how did you get here?" Gavin queried.

"I took a taxi," explained Thomas cheerily. "It would have taken me much longer if I had cycled like you. I just had to find out what was going on."

"Where did you get the money to pay for it?" Gavin wondered.

"Oh, that was easy," chirped Thomas. "I found some in the box you keep beside your bed. And don't worry, I gave the taxi driver a good tip."

Gavin looked as though he would like to give Thomas more than a good tip. What they called in the old days a *buffet* was suggesting itself to him. At this juncture, however, Gustavus spoke.

"Would you two mind telling me what you're doing here?" he said.

Like the prosecutor in a television programme who is about to cross-examine a witness, Gavin strode forward, the Form Year Book under his arm.

"How," he asked, displaying two pages of photographs, "do you explain this?"

Gustavus Wilkins looked at the photograph.

"Oh!" he said. "I never thought anyone looked at those books. Otherwise I would have taken care of it."

"Spill, Wilkins," instructed Thomas. "The game's up."

"To what game are you referring?" enquired Gustavus loftily.

"You know what he means," said Gavin meaningfully. "The photographs of you in every year."

"They're not photographs of me," explained Gustavus unconvincingly. "It's just that each year there was someone who looked like me in the class. Handsome chaps they were too."

"No," said Gavin. "Won't do."

Gustavus sat down on a chair behind his bench. He sighed.

"Perhaps I had better tell you," he said. "I could, of course, wipe your memories of all this. But, just now, I find myself in need of help."

Chapter Three

"I am," commenced Gustavus, "an orphan."

"You are not, " snapped Gavin disbelievingly. "Your mother let me in."

"That," said Gustavus, "was not my mother. That was what we magicians call an *eidolon*. It is merely an image of a human being. I keep it to answer the door, to avoid suspicious persons or, worse still, hostile beings. It doesn't have any reality. It is not there. It just appears to be there. You'll notice it didn't speak a lot. It isn't really capable of continuous conversation."

"This is getting dead good," muttered Thomas.

"What do you mean, *we magicians*?" questioned Gavin.

"Let me get on with my story," said Gustavus, producing a banana from his pocket and absent-mindedly peeling it. "I was an orphan. I was raised until I was nine years old in an orphanage. It was called the Good Hope Orphanage or, to use its official name, the Good Hope Residential Care Home for Minors and it was the greatest dump south of the River Thames. The Staff were horrible and cruel or, in the case of the pleasanter ones, just horrible. It was a place that would have frightened Charles Dickens. I don't know how it managed to survive in modern times. Everybody got bullied except the bullies and even they had been bullied when they were younger. The staff consisted of careworkers who were so appalling it was clear they would never have got jobs anywhere else. Most would have benefited from visits to Alcoholics Anonymous, Weight Watchers and a shop that sold nicotine patches. At age nine, I, Gustavus Wilkins, decided to run away. I don't believe my disappearance was ever reported to anyone. I suspect it was just covered up."

He took a thoughtful bite from his banana.

"After two days travel across country, I was feeling hungry. People speak of adventurers' *living off the land.* Exactly how they do it, I don't know, for there isn't much on the land to live off, unless you like eating grass and mud. I drank a couple of times from streams, but I had nothing to eat. I decided I would have to kill a sheep and eat that. The sheep objected to being killed and chased me away at my first attempt. I didn't know sheep could be so fierce. Then I saw in the distance a house. Maybe, if I asked for food they would give me some. I went up and knocked upon the door.

An old and ferocious lady with a walking stick answered and, when she discovered I was looking for food she gave me a wallop with the stick which I can still feel. She also used unbecoming language. I hastened away. But, at the next house, I was luckier.

This was answered by a housekeeper and it transpired that she too had, as a child, been in the Good Hope Orphanage. She knew exactly what I was running away from. She had every sympathy. Her name was Mrs Jarvis. She was actually quite young - in her twenties, I would have said. She invited me in and called out, 'Professor Vilnius, we have a visitor.'

So it was that for the first time I met Professor Petroc Vilnius, Litt.D., D.Phil. It was quite a while before I discovered that he was a Professor Emeritus, which means a retired professor who doesn't profess any more. He had a round smiley face, rather like the smiley faces you get on computers, except that he had a nose, which they don't. He also had a short beard. Funnily, though, his body was round also, though on a larger scale. I won't say he was fat, but he was certainly not undernourished. He greeted me affably. He knew the Good Hope Orphanage by repute.

'Mrs Jarvis has told me all about that woeful place,' he said sympathetically. Hearing that I had been wandering the countryside, a meal was offered at once.

'It so happens,' he said, after I had finished my repast, 'that I am in need of an assistant around here. A sort of general bottle-washer to assist Mrs Jarvis, as you can see she isn't getting any younger. [*Snort of indignation from Mrs Jarvis*]. You could handle the job very well. I could pay you a small salary, plus board and lodging. I could also arrange for you to attend the local school, which is aspiring to reach a standard of mediocrity in the education it provides, shackled as it is by the strictures of the Department of Education and Science. Do you think such an arrangement would suit you?' Well, obviously, this was a good step up from the Good Hope Orphanage, so I accepted with alacrity.

As the months passed, I discovered Professor Vilnius, though he might not be professing any longer, was certainly working at something. His house was quite large and there were some rooms in it which were out of bounds. Mrs Jarvis was allowed to go in there to tidy and assured me they contained nothing mysterious. The Professor always insisted, despite her youth, on addressing her formally as Mrs Jarvis, to preserve professionalism. She insisted I call her Katy and, as we had both the experience of the Orphanage, we became quite pally. She brought me home for Sunday lunch one day, as she lived nearby. I was astonished to discover that her husband, who was named Ben, was a clergyman. He was a very learned type of clergyman too, rather old fashioned. He told me about how he had met Katy.

'I was advised by the Bishop to marry,' he said, 'for, in the Church of England, it increases your chance of promotion. I hadn't a clue whom to marry, as every young lady in my small country parish tended to head for the bright lights of the city on reaching marriageable age. Then I thought of the Orphanage - dreadful place, I knew, for I had reported it several times only to have my reports ignored by civil servants. *Orphanages,* I thought, *generally kick out young girls when they're more or less grown up. I wonder if there are any eligible ones there at present?*

So thither I went. Mr Rumball, the man in charge, was highly suspicious of me, thinking I might be a government inspector, but when I told him my problem, he immediately said there were four girls of the age of sixteen about to leave with no place to go. (Something should have been organized for them, but that wouldn't have bothered old Rumball.) Any one of them would be glad to find someone who would offer her a home and a chance to settle down. A home was what all of them had missed for most of their lives. When I spoke to the four I chose Katy straight away, as she was the only one who wasn't a drug addict, and we were married shortly afterwards. Katy, after the awful life she had undergone, was only too happy to find someone who would treat her kindly. The Bishop was not altogether happy about the arrangement, but when I told him it had been either that or computer dating he accepted things.

The Bishop has always been distrustful of anything acquired through computers."

"Look, Wilkins," said Gavin, growing impatient, "fascinating as this Mills and Boone saga may be, could we get back to you and your multiple pictures?"

Gustavus took another bite of his banana.

"Hold your horses, I'm getting there," he said grumpily. "One day the Prof - I had come to address him as Prof - told me that he was engaged in very special work. 'Have you ever heard,' he said, 'of the Wand of Merlin?' I replied that I hadn't, but at a guess I reckoned it was a wand Merlin had used.

'It is said that when King Arthur fought his final battle in the year 542 or thereabouts, he was taken to the land of Avalon by Morgan La Fée to recover from his wounds and it was believed that one day he would return when the land needed him.'

'I thought Morgan La Fée was a baddie,' I said, for I had read some Arthurian tales.

'Not in the original story,' said the Prof. 'The French romancers made her into Arthur's enemy, but in the original sources she was his ally. She belonged to a very powerful race of beings whom the Ancient Britons thought were gods. They weren't, but they were a great deal more powerful than humans. The island of Avalon was in fact a parallel universe where her people lived. There are a number of entrances, one of them being on the Tor at Glastonbury. It was there she took Arthur and there he remains.

'Afterwards Merlin, who had never been too stable in the first place, went mad at the Battle of Arthuret and, among other things, he lost his wand. Now the magic Merlin practised and the magic of Morgan's people was not evil magic involving demons, which is very dangerous and should be avoided at all costs. It is making use of laws of nature which men haven't discovered yet and which are as unknown to the human race as was electricity to our ancestors. Indeed, Gustaus, I was thinking of taking you on as an apprentice, training you in the arts of natural magic. Anyway, Merlin's wand was charged with vast quantities of this magic, enough to blow up cities and reduce millions of men to destruction. The wizards of the day had to find it for safety's sake. Well, it was found and buried it in a casket lined with orichalc, a metal difficult to discover, which had been used in Atlantis, but which is now found no more. One of our number had had a small store of it. This casket was buried on Richill in Sussex and there we hoped it would remain, at least until Arthur's return. Some years ago, however, the town of Hillford grew larger in size - a glass factory and two car factories swelled the population. The Richill area was built over and, on Richill itself, they built a school. Now, because there are so many people about, we fear for the Wand. There are many unscrupulous people who know about it and would use it for their evil designs, should they discover its whereabouts We need to appoint a guardian there.'

It was then he proposed to me that I go there as a pupil to keep my eye on what was going on, to make sure nobody was digging up any of the school grounds (for it is housed in a large underground chamber) to ensure nobody suspicious looking was hanging about asking questions or the like. It appeared that various persons of evil intent would like to get their hands on the Wand, but didn't know its location. Each year I would join the same class. They would freeze my age. I was now twelve and I would grow no older. They would wipe the memories of those at the school so they wouldn't know I had been in your class the year before. I have now been there for ten years. Although I have lived for twenty-two years, I am still, in all that counts, a twelve year old. I have, in addition, learned quite a bit of magic. The memories of those in school, both staff and pupils, are wiped every year, so every year they think I am a new pupil. Dr Cudgell is given a false memory each year which makes him think he has interviewed my parents and accepted me as a pupil. The only thing we didn't think of was the photographs in the Form Year Books."

On hearing all of this, Gavin and Thomas let out long breaths. They couldn't believe what they have heard. But there was more to come.

Chapter Four

"Do you remember," said Gustavus with a sigh, "those telephone men?"

"No," said Gavin. "What telephone men?"

"You must remember," said Gustavus. "Dr Cudgell warned us at assembly that they were coming to put a new landline in. He told us to keep out of their way. I thought nothing of it at the time. Then I caught the flu."

"Yes, I remember the flu outbreak," said Gavin. "I tried to convince Mother I had it. She wasn't having any of it."

"Your trouble is you look too healthy," piped up Thomas. "Your trouble is you lack pallor. Pallor is what every dodger needs. Pallor might be labelled the schoolboy's friend."

"What I hadn't realised is that these supposed telephone men were laying an underground landline, so it wouldn't get blown down in a storm. This meant they had to dig up the ground. They must have found the underground chamber and from it they took the Wand. When I returned to school, I went into the chamber - I knew where the secret entrance is - and the Wand was gone. I tried to check up on the telephone company and found out from Miss Bilton that they were a new company that offered cheap lines with extra-fast broadband. But when they left, the men hadn't completed their work and when Dr

Cudgell tried phoning their office, he discovered it was a non-existent company. He alerted the police, but they were at a loss, especially as the fake company hadn't extracted any money from the school."

Miss Bilton, I should tell you, was the school secretary. School secretaries are generally the epitome of discretion - they will never talk to the children about school business. But Miss Bilton was the exception. If she had a juicy secret, she could never resist the temptation to unload it. It had been quite easy for Gustavus to find out the truth from her.

"When I told the Professor," continued Gustavus, "he said to wait for further instructions."

"And did these instructions, further as they were, arrive?" Thomas wondered.

"I'm still waiting for them," said Gustavus miserably. Although he might have weathered two and twenty summers, Gustavus looked like a very downcast 12-year old boy. He would have felt like one too.

"He did say that he had a fair idea who was behind it all," Gustavus continued. "Whoever it was probably knew the value of the Wand, as nothing else in the chamber was taken, even though there was a sword with a jewel-encrusted hilt, a small tiara and other quite valuable gewgaws."

"How did the thieves know where the Wand was buried?" wondered Gavin.

"That," said Gustavus, "is anybody's guess."

"No, it is not," chirped Thomas. "It is my guess and my guess is that someone else who knew where it was buried tipped these evildoers off."

"But who, apart from the Prof, would know where it was?" Gustavus demanded.

"You said he spoke of other wizards that he was clearly working with," said Gavin. "Perhaps one of them tipped him off."

"Well done, Gavin," said Thomas. "Sherlock Holmes would gasp at your powers of deduction. Is this Professor in some kind of organisation of wizards or do they form a loose alliance? Are others - non-wizards - involved with him as well? Speak, Wilkins, and enlighten us."

"Did your brother at some stage swallow a dictionary?" Gustavus asked Gavin.

"He's always been like that," Gavin replied.

There came a quick burst of *The Ride of the Valkyries*. It was Gustavus' mobile. He picked it up. Taking it into a corner, he muttered for a few minutes. Then, switching off, he said, "That was the Prof. He's coming here from Pulborough later in the day. I had to tell him you had found out what was going on. He said he would have to speak to you as well. Can you make it back here for four o'clock?"

They could. Thomas and Gavin quitted the house.

"Did all that happen for real?" wondered Gavin, who, now that they were outside in the real world, was beginning to find it just a little bit difficult to believe all he had heard in the last short while.

"Certainly, brother mine," said Thomas. "We have landed in the midst of an adventure strange and marvellous. Goodness knows where it will lead. I want a biscuit."

It was with biscuit eating in mind that our two heroes reached the gateway of their home, but before they reached the front door, next door's front door opened and from it, leaping like a gazelle, came Caroline, who was brimming with eagerness to hear the outcome of their investigations into the strange case of Gustavus Wilkins.

"Did you tell her about it?" demanded Gavin, with a sour look.

"She forced me," lied Thomas. "I could not resist the power of her strangling hands."

"I'll give you strangling hands in a minute," growled Caroline. "You guys are gonna spill."

She knew so much of the mystery that Gavin reckoned it would be foolish to leave the story of their visit to Gustavus untold. She would only get curious and a curious female, as many of my readers well know, can be a menace to secrecy. Gavin invited her in and, over squash and biscuits, unfolded the story Gustavus had told them, leaving out the romantic adventures of Ben the vicar, which he felt were superfluous.

Caroline was an imaginative person. Otherwise, I fear she might have had difficulty in swallowing Gavin's story with the same gusto as she swallowed the biscuits. You could see her eyes light up with excitement.

"I'm coming with you at four o'clock," she informed them.

It was then they heard the front door open.

There shouldn't have been anyone coming home at that hour. Gavin and Thomas exchanged apprehensive glances. Then they heard a humming sound. It was not unlike the Humming Chorus from *Madame Butterfly*. This was because it was the Humming Chorus from *Madame Butterfly*, only not being hummed very well. Around the corner came the humming figure of Father.

The presence of children had obviously not crossed Father's mind. It was not impossible he had forgotten he had any. And it was certainly a surprise to him to find them at home. Remember, this was the first day of the school holidays and usually at this hour the house would have been deserted, except for Mother writing her magazine articles.

"Oh!" said Father. "I didn't expect to find you here. Mother has been interviewing a celebrity named Samson Strange and apparently she's bringing him home for a meal this evening. She's just phoned me to say she wants me to tidy up the place. You can help."

"Well, I'll see you both at, say, half past three," announced Caroline, rising to her feet. She had certainly no wish to be roped in to a tidying up operation.

Although Caroline lived next door, it was clear Father had no idea of who she was and he watched her departure with a slight look of puzzlement in his eyes.

There then followed a frenzy of tidying up. Father did most of the frenzying, instructing the boys to pick up this, remove that, find the Hoover, use the Hoover, get the dust off that window sill and do the breakfast dishes. They found a particularly sticky piece of chewing gum attached to the underside of a chair, the television remote down behind a cushion and a bishop under the sofa. (The bishop was a chess piece). Thomas discovered a long-lost exercise book, dog eared and dog chewed, wedged behind a waste basket and Father decided he had better clean up the bathroom so he bounded up the stairs and at last gave his exhausted offspring some peace. The family dog, Rover, had taken refuge in his basket, over the edge of which he had stared with disapproving eyes at the turmoil.

At about three thirty Caroline entered through the back door.

"Have you guys finished tidying up?" she asked carefully.

They said they had. Father had returned to his office, a look of relief on his face. Caroline was having some doubts about the whole enterprise they were involved in.

"Are you sure about Wilkins?" she demanded. "I mean, his whole story sounds kinda crazy."

"We have the evidence of the photographs," reminded Gavin.

"And don't forget that cool gun thing," added Thomas.

"Also," said Gavin, "he didn't sound as if he were lying. There was too much detail in his story."

"I'd agree, Brother," said Thomas. "It is a well-known fact that a false story lacks detail."

"Well, let's get out of here then," said Caroline.

Gavin and Caroline had bicycles. Thomas sat on Gavin's crossbar. I shall not bore you with details of their journey to Gustavus' house.

"Does this guy Wilkins act like a grownup or a twelve-year old?" Caroline wondered.

"I didn't see anything particularly grown up about him," said Thomas. "But he's a bit fat. You could say he's a *grown-out* rather than a grown-up."

They arrived at Gustavus' house and knocked upon the door. It was answered by the vague-looking woman who, Gustavus had said, wasn't really there and, now that they knew, she looked less there than she had the last time. Thomas even fancied that he could actually see *through* her.

Gustavus came out of the chamber at the back of the house. He ushered them into it and, for the first time, all saw Professor Petroc Vilnius.

He didn't look professorial at all. He had a round and pleasant face and the rest of him was fairly round too. I think *rotund* is the word I am looking for. He wore an upper garment that looked like a cross between a shirt and a sweater. It was unusual, but not so unusual that it would cause comment if he were walking down the street in it. His eyes did not have the penetrating glance which you might expect of a run of the mill professor, nor the vague glance you might expect of an absent-minded professor. In fact, his eyes twinkled.

"Come in and sit down," he said. "Gustavus, you mentioned two boys had become involved, but you said nothing about a young lady."

"There wasn't a young lady this morning," said Gustavus, scratching his ear. "I don't know who she is. She doesn't go to our school."

Caroline went to an expensive international school which mainly catered for the children of foreign business executives living in London. The companies they worked for paid the fees.

"Well, a boy who talks too much told her about this," said Gavin, casting a sour look at Thomas.

"I admit I talk too much," said Thomas. "It's brought on by the strain of having an overbearing brother."

"Never mind," said Professor Vilnius. "It can't be helped. However, I don't like children being brought into this. You have found yourselves in the middle of something which involves some very dangerous people. Come to me, cheese sandwich."

There had been a plate of cheese sandwiches in the centre of the table. One of them flew out and landed in the Professor's hand. He thoughtfully took a bite.

"You have all, I am sure, heard of Stonehenge, called in former time the Giants' Dance," began the Prof. "Way back, in prehistoric times, it was part of the realm of a king called Golar. King Golar's realm was invaded by beings who emerged from the sea; but, while they could live under the sea, they could also exist with equal ease upon the land. They were led by a creature who was called Demogorgon. He was like a giant octopus, except he had ten tentacles rather than eight and a mouthful of huge and yellow fangs. His followers were creatures with seaweed-like hair and a generally humanoid shape. Well, King Golar, as one might well expect, opposed him. But King Golar's weapons were fashioned with bronze, while the host of Demogorgon had weapons wrought of some unknown metal to be found beneath the bed of the sea. They also had ray-guns of a type and King Golar's warriors had no chance against them.

King Golar, having seen his men overcome in battle, knew there was only one way to deal with these creatures and that was by magic. He went to Cargolian, the Amethyst Wizard, so called because he had once lost an arm and had a replacement wrought of amethyst. Said he, 'There is but one way to defeat these seaborn warriors and that is to loose the Beasts of Gurgoid upon them.'. He directed the king to the mountains of what we today call Scotland where these animals lived. He took his most skilled hunters with him and they captured four of these creatures. They were huge in extent and resembled in shape nothing so much as pancakes. Their only features were tiny eyes and huge mouths. They could never have been captured had not Cargolian, who had accompanied the expedition, bespelled them, rendering them drowsy and inactive. These were brought down to the seashore and set free. Drowsy no longer, they slithered forth and breathed and the foulness of their breath caused the forces of Demogorgon to fall in scores and in hundreds. But Demogorgon was not so easy a proposition to deal with. As the four Beasts of Gurgoid entered the water and submerged, he directed from his mouth a blast which blew forty of Golar's followers to fragments, so that all fled.

The wizard Cargolian, however, was unflurried. 'Wait until the coming of eventide,' he told the King. 'Then will our foe seek to drink.' And, as the wizard had said, with the onset of twilight the horrid Demogorgon made his way to a nearby river and quaffed the water. But the wizard had drugged the water with a powerful drug and Demogorgon sank into a deep sleep.

'Now,' said the wizard, 'Demogorgon cannot be killed. But there is a hill nearby which opens into a small, prison-like dimension. Take him there, lock him away.'

This they did. The hauled the horrid wet mass that was Demogorgon across the grassland and opened the portal and into this they stuffed him and sealed it tightly.

'Now,' said the wizard, 'he can never get out unless certain rites are enacted. Certain spells must be pronounced and a princess, a direct descendant of you, King Golar, must be sacrificed at the Rock of Gastry. But as century follows century your line will be forgotten and none will know who your direct descendants are. Demogorgon is sealed in forever.'

The years passed and hundreds of years and thousands of years and King Golar slipped even from the memory of man - or so it was thought. But Demogorgon had followers who had summoned him ashore in the first place. When these died, other generations took their place. Their plan was to restore Demogorgon. So powerful was he, they wished him to conquer the whole earth. They could not hope to keep track of King Golar's descendants so one of them wove a spell - that every female descendant of his line would have a birthmark, shaped like a star, on her shoulder. The star would be of an unusual shade, a colour not found in this dimension, and this would enable them to discover her.

As these people thought they would, they lost track of Golar's line. But now, things have changed. They have discovered the Wand of Merlin and stolen it from the school grounds, which gives them the world's most powerful weapon, and they have found a female descendant of Golar to sacrifice. They will bring the hideous demon back. They plan soon to bring the world under their sway and I fear only the Council of Wizards can stop them.'

"Where does this Council of Wizards operate from?" asked Gavin.

"Alas, they do not," sighed the Prof. "I, Petroc Vilnius, am the only operational wizard at present. Pothinus the Wise is so old he can barely move and he lives his life these days in Florida, whither he has repaired for the climate. Dzang of Tibet went into the Himalayas and has not been seen since. Rumour has it that he has become a *lung-gom-pa* or entranced runner. Anvard the dwarf went into the regions beneath the earth and has not been seen for many summers. Udaun the leprechaun is under an enchantment. So you see how dangerous all this is. I am the only one left who can stem the tide of the Order of Demogorgon. They are led by an individual known as the Shapeshifter, who goes amongst humans under many aliases. The whole situation is fraught with peril. I cannot let children become involved. You must forget that all this happened. I do not wish to wipe your memories, but, if you continue to be involved, that is what I shall have to do."

He stood up to indicate the interview was at an end and that he was about to lead them to the door. Suddenly, he collapsed upon the floor. There he lay, unconscious.

Chapter Five

As you can imagine, this more than startled the children. Caroline, who was efficient, knelt down and felt his pulse "He's still alive," she said.

"Has he been zapped by enemies?" wondered Thomas.

Gustavus was on his mobile, ringing for an ambulance.

"I don't think so," said Gavin. "This looks like a heart attack or maybe a stroke to me."

It seemed to take an eternity for the ambulance to arrive, but in fact it was less than ten minutes. Thomas gave the Prof a few pokes to see if he could induce any signs of life, but Gavin stopped him. When the ambulance arrived, the paramedics placed their portly patient on a stretcher while one of them asked Gustavus who he was and where they might find his next of kin.

"His name is Petroc Vilnius," informed Gustavus. "He lives near Pulborough. I don't think he has a next of kin. You might get in touch with Mrs Jarvis, his housekeeper. She's the Vicar's wife."

The ambulance sped off towards Hillford General Hospital leaving a group of nonplussed youngsters in its wake.

"What do we do now?" wondered Gavin.

"There's only one thing to do," said Gustavus solemnly. "It's up to us to defeat the Order of Demogorgon. We have to find where their leader the Shapeshifter is and also this Princess they've tracked down."

"And how do you suppose we're going to do that?" Caroline demanded.

Thomas already had the answer.

"By guile and stealth," he proposed.

"That's a rather vague recipe," observed Gustavus with a smile. He was rather taken with Thomas's turns of phrase. "I suggest you all go home while I have a think about the matter. We can meet here again tomorrow."

"Can we have some of those cool zap guns Gavin told me about?" requested Thomas.

"I have only one of those and here it stays. Those things are far too dangerous to give to people who aren't used to handling them."

Thomas looked disappointed.

"We'll have to get back for tea anyway," said Gavin. "Mother's bringing some celebrity guest home and she'll have a hairy canary if we're not there."

So it was the three cyclists set off for home.

"What's Samson Strange famous for anyway?" demanded Thomas from the crossbar. "I've never heard of him."

"He's a poet. He visited our school once and read his poetry," informed Caroline. "He's one of these modern poets who writes a lot of grot and everyone says it's major art."

The way back from Tandem Street was mainly downhill. The Gripe in particular was an easy ride. In fact, the bicycles speeded up rather worryingly as they approached its base. I am happy to report, however, that all arrived home safely.

"Well, good luck with your poet," wished Caroline.

They entered the house. Neither Father nor Mother, much less Samson Strange, had arrived yet. They did not, however, have to wait long. First Father turned up. He advanced on an armchair, plunged into it and opened a book on statistics. It was called *Statistics*. The author was the celebrated mathematician A.K. Biddlecombe. If you love mathematics and especially statistics, A.K. Biddlecombe is the man for you. His books will make you shudder with delight. The door opened.

The art of making an entrance was obviously something that Samson Strange had practised and practised well. He was a man of six feet with a great mop of white hair and a long white beard. His face was middle-aged and craggy. He wore a neckerchief, an upper garment which might be termed a tunic and a pair of jeans which were tucked into long high heeled boots. On coming in he stretched his hands above his head, rather as you would if a gun were pointed at you, and proclaimed, "This house is a delight. Such furnishings! Such *objets d'art*! Such taste!"

Gavin looked first at this apparition and then around the room at the rather shabby sofa and the chairs with lived-in and sat-on coverings. In fact, Mother was always going on about getting a leather suite, a fact that made Father hide behind his newspaper in even firmer fashion. Were those two vases with giraffes painted on them what Samson Strange meant by *objets d'art* ? He supposed so. Father put down his book and approached Samson Strange with faltering footsteps. The poet stuck out a large hand.

"Mr Taylor, meeting you is a pleasure," he cried. "Your lovely wife has already treated me to a delicious lunch and now she has offered me the pleasure of a home-cooked meal. I salivate already," he boomed.

Father, looking greatly as though he wished he were somewhere else, took Samson Strange's large hand. Mother then came in, carrying a bag of comestibles she had picked up on the way home.

"Why don't I get you both a nice glass of sherry while I prepare the meal?" she asked.

The two men sat on the sofa, Father doing this rather gingerly, because if you sat too heavily on that sofa parts of its innards came outwards. Samson Strange, not even thinking of such things, threw himself onto it and there was the sound of a possibly breaking spring as he did so. Each accepted his glass of sherry and Mother repaired to the kitchen.

If the truth be told, Mother was not a dab-hand at cookery. But she knew where you could buy ready-made meals that were indistinguishable from home-cooked foods. This interview with Samson Strange was going to make her career and it was vital she impress him. The ready-made meal had cost an arm and a leg, but it would be worth it if it led to his trumpeting her skills in artistic circles. A little bit of this and a little bit of that, some Worcestershire sauce and some herbs and spices were added to her pre-prepared goulash and all was ready. The table had already been set by Father during his earlier visit home. It was not long before she informed one and all that dinner was served.

When the meal had been served, Samson Strange brayed in a loud voice, "Ah, I see this is the kind of goulash that takes its name from the Szekely people. Just what the doctor ordered. I am no lover of potatoes, Catherine, my dear, and I find sauerkraut and sour cream much more palatable." Samson Strange obviously knew his goulashes. In case you haven't worked it out, Catherine was Mother's name. She wrote her magazine articles under the name of Catherine von Sturm, as she felt Catherine Taylor was too bland and her maiden name of Catherine Pobbles too unsophisticated.

The meal being over, Samson Strange said in his thunderous voice, "Perhaps you would like me to read my latest poem."

His latest poem had not been published yet and to hear it and write comments about it would certainly be a feather in Mother's cap. She acquiesced enthusiastically, Father said "Uh!" and the boys felt they would never get away from the table.

Samson Strange stood up and took from an attaché case a single sheet of paper. He cleared his throat and read the title "*Farts of Doom*". Thomas promptly had to pretend he was choking to cover the laughter the title produced. Gavin was about to snigger, but Mother kicked him under the table.

"Are you all right, young man?" asked Samson Strange solicitously as Father slapped Thomas on the back. Thomas took a mouthful of water and said he was. The Great Poet then read:

> *Twice-snorting swine berate the ether*
> *Gasps of infinity tread upon the finite*
> *Galoshes are no more effective*
> *The dentures of the odious ply their task*
> *The doodlesack is sounded in Glencoe*
> *We have no handkerchief*
> *And fools call out for Philomel.*

This was obviously the end of the piece, for Samson Strange looked around with a big grin that was obviously expectant of appreciation. Mother immediately started to gush. She proclaimed it a wonderful work, its imagery so evocative of the state of modern man. Father, who generally looked upon the world with puzzlement, was filled with utter confusion. The two boys were filled with the hope that Samson Strange was going to read no more of his magna opera. Happily, he was not. However, when Mother invited him to stay the night and he accepted, Father blenched.

The boys had had a tiring day and were quite pleased when bedtime came. Gavin could hear the loud sound of Samson Strange downstairs, regaling his parents with goodness knows what pretentious drivel. Soon Gavin fell asleep. It was in the middle of the night that he woke up.

Chapter Six

Gavin was awoken by the most appalling animal screech he had ever heard. It was not the cry of a cat or the howl of a dog. It was a scream of its own type, a ghastly, eerie, terrifying wail that seemed to rend the very air outside in two. It terrified Gavin so much that at first he was afraid to look out of the window to see what had made this atrocious noise. But then it was repeated again and again and he felt he just had to see what could make this stomach-turning sound, which rose to a hideous crescendo as he approached the window.

The moon was high in the sky and the garden was lit almost as well as it was by day. There, standing in the middle of it, was the most peculiar beast he had ever observed. No zoo he had ever visited had been tenanted by such an extraordinary creature. It was the size of a leopard and had a coat of long brown fur, but the fur was patchy and the skin of parts of its body, scabrous and disgusting, was visible. Indeed, it seemed the skin was diseased and decaying. The head of the animal he could not clearly see, as the beast had its back to him. It was lean in shape and the ears were small and triangular. As he watched it, it screamed once more and voided its bowels on the grassy garden. Then Gavin saw something else in the garden next door.

Advancing from the house was Mr Blackman, carrying a single-barrelled shotgun. He was advancing slowly, lest the slightest noise should betray his approach. He raised the gun and aimed it at the animal.

In case you are not familiar with firearms, I would mention that shotguns do not fire bullets. A shotgun fires a cartridge which opens and sends a bunch of pellets towards its target. Mr Blackman took aim and fired, but his hands were shaking. Most of the pellets missed their mark, but a few hit the beast in its right back leg. The noise to which it gave vent I cannot describe. It was an unbelievable scream and, before his astonished eyes, Gavin saw his window pane crack. Mr Blackman was not staying around to try another shot. He ran like fury for the shelter of his abode and Gavin himself, terrified by what he had seen and heard, zoomed back into his bed and concealed himself beneath the bedclothes.

Later that night, there was knocking at the door. Gavin heard the sound of Father shuffling down the stairs to answer it. It was the police and a couple of men with nets. The police told Father that his neighbour had reported a wild animal in his back garden. Father, who was a deep sleeper, hadn't heard anything. The police included men with rifles. They went out back and could find no beast, but they remarked upon a pile of steaming ordure at one place.

"Better bag that and take it for analysis," said Sergeant Pratchett to Constable Baxter.

Constable Baxter was not overjoyed by being assigned this duty, but complied.

Next morning Gavin, who had been sleeping badly, made his way to Thomas's room. Thomas was already awake. He too had heard the noises, but had deemed it politic to remain in his bed.

They went downstairs to breakfast. Coming down the stairs after them was Samson Strange. Gavin noted he was limping with his right leg.

Chapter Seven

Breakfast was not what might be described as an interesting meal. Mother produced a cooked breakfast, thinking the presence of Samson Strange merited that. Neither Gavin nor Thomas really fancied kidneys at that hour of the morning and Mother had overcooked the bacon, so that it was spotted black in places. The eggs ran like Alph the sacred river. Father felt he could not read the paper when he had a guest. He had slept through the uproar the previous night. I suppose he had a pristine conscience. Mother had not slept through it, but once Mother was in bed for the night, there she stayed. Nothing short of a volcanic eruption underneath the house would get her out of bed, whatever bizarre noises she heard. However, the boys brought the matter of the night's doings up.

"I didn't hear anything," boomed Samson Strange. "Animals, gunshots and police - there was I, fast asleep. I put it down to your comfortable mattresses, Catherine, my dear. Gavin, would you please pass the salt?"

"It was like some strange mystery animal howling." observed Gavin. "I've never heard anything like it in the zoo."

"You'll have to tell the cryptozoologists," said Samson Strange. "They're people who look for mystery animals like the Loch Ness Monster and Bigfoot."

After breakfast Samson Strange bade his adieux.

"If any of you ever pass my house outside Petworth, do drop in," he invited. "I have found my little stay with you an inspiration - an inspiration indeed."

"Have you hurt your leg?" asked Thomas innocently, referring to his limp.

"Yes, must have twisted a muscle during the night," replied the poet. "Once you reach a certain age, you know, you lose the pliability of youth. And now farewell."

The boys wandered back into the kitchen. Caroline came in through the back door.

"Caroline, I wish you would come through the front door and knock," said Mother crossly. "This isn't your house, you know."

"But I always come in through your backyard," protested Caroline.

"I wish you wouldn't call it a *yard*," said Mother peevishly. "It calls to mind a farmyard, with hens and pigs and other insanitary things wandering about it."

"Sorry, Mrs T., we always call back gardens backyards back home," said Caroline. "I can assure you I didn't see a single pig or even half a hen."

Mother and Father made their usual departures, taking thirty seconds (Father) and ten minutes (Mother). As soon as they were gone, Caroline eyeballed Gavin.

"What was all that ruckus about last night?" she said. "I could hear an animal that seemed deranged in your backyard. Then a gunshot. I got out of bed to have a look, but I couldn't see over that leylandii hedge that grows along between the houses."

They unfolded the story of their strange guest of the night before.

"I told you he was a gruzzle" said Caroline. "But you cannot be serious about him limping after this animal had been shot in the leg. I mean, you make it sound like he was a shapeshifter or something."

She suddenly realised what she had said.

"A *shapeshifter*! Let's go see Wilkins."

****

The Good Hope Orphanage is not the most pleasant care home in the south of England. In fact, it is probably by far the worst and how the Powers That Be continued to let it operate demands investigation. It was now officially called a Residential Home rather than an Orphanage, but the locals still called it an orphanage. The proprietor, Josias Rumball, was not a pleasant looking man, either. His chin was always coated with stubble. I would call it designer stubble, except there wasn't much evidence of design. Now in his late fifties, he had a look of sloth and lethargy and even decay about him. By day he sat in a leather chair behind a desk. From this leather chair he rarely moved. On the desk was a computer, which he seldom employed for purposes of work. There was also a leather-bound notebook in which he kept a list of glib phrases for fobbing people off. A bottle of whisky reposed in one of the drawers in his desk. Shortly before midday, there came a knock on his door. Mr

Rumball frowned. He had been using the Internet to place bets and did not want to be interrupted. He switched the screen to a social services site and barked, "Come in!"

A tall, suave stranger dressed in black entered. He had an elegance about him that was quite the opposite of the demeanour of the poet who had visited the Taylors. Whereas the latter had looked rugged and tough, this man looked sophisticated and urbane and a good deal younger. Rumball sat up. The atmosphere in the room changed. It was clear that Rumball regarded this person with no small trepidation. His visitor carried a silver-topped cane and wore a dark suit, which really looked as though it belonged in 19th Century Paris. He had a black top hat, which he laid on Rumball's desk. His voice was smooth, silky, almost like an anaesthetic.

"My dear Rumball, good morning, I hope you are well. It is, after all, a pleasant day. Not a cloud in the sky. So unusual for an English summer, *n'est-ce pas?* May I sit down?"

" 'Course. 'Course you can, guvnor," said Rumball, at the same time sitting up and trying to look attentive, even though a couple of shots from the whisky bottle not long before had somewhat befuddled his mind.

"I had been meaning to call on you to see if you had still been able to keep a Certain Person under observation since you let her go at age sixteen. Yes, yes, I know you had no choice. The law, my dear Rumball, is, after all, the law. There would have been serious consequences had you forced her to remain here and your little scheme for keeping her at an observable location was nothing short of ingenious. She has not strayed, I take it?" Mr Rumball gazed at his visitor's clean-shaven chin, jet black hair and handlebar moustache.

"No, indeed, Mr Etrange, I would of told you immediate," he reassured him.

"How nice," said the visitor in his soft, soporific tones. "We shall need her soon, you see. By the way, if anyone called *Taylor* turns up here or gets in touch with you in any way, I should like to be informed."

"Well, I ain't seen anyone o' that name recent," Mr Rumball reassured him. "Mind you, there was a man called Tinker as used to work here as a handyman, but he cut orf his hand with a power tool and he ain't so handy now, I'll tell you."

"Fascinating," said the visitor with a languid yawn. "You'll excuse me, I had a somewhat disturbed night. Now, Mr Rumball, I trust you know that without my support you would not be able to keep this sinkhole of an establishment open for two minutes, so heed my instructions carefully."

The visitor arose and departed. Mr Rumball noted that he was limping slightly.

****

Mr Blackman was unhappy. He had found the creature he had shot and wounded last night quite terrifying. He was telling his wife, Janice, about it for the fortieth time.

"Look, Wellington," she said, "each time you tell me about this animal, it's grown a metre in length and developed additional tusks."

"I never said it had tusks," protested Mr Blackman.

"I was reading in the newspaper about people called Crippled Zoologists who study mystery animals. Why don't you ring them up and see if they can identify what you saw."

Mr Blackman frowned. Perhaps not a bad idea, he thought. By doing an Internet search, he came on the Worthing Cryptozoology Society. He discovered that they investigated reports of mystery black cats, alleged lake monsters and other things of that nature. He decided to give them a call.

Chapter Eight

When the Taylors and Caroline arrived at Gustavus Wilkins' house, the latter was just back from visiting the hospital. Dr Petroc Vilnius was not a well man. He was conscious, but not very conscious. He had grunted to Gustavus that it was now up to him to frustrate the followers of Demogorgon.

"They won't proceed without the Wand and the princess to sacrifice," he gasped. "You'll have to get the Wand back."

The medicos were not sure what was the matter with Dr Vilnius. They were conducting tests.

The children told Gustavus about Samson Strange and how they feared he might be the Shapeshifter.

"I don't see why he should come to your house to be interviewed by your mother," mused Gustavus. "This interview must have been arranged some time ago. You lot weren't involved in all this until yesterday."

"Well," said Gavin slowly, "isn't it possible he discovered by some magic means that we *would* become involved? Knowing that, he arranged the interview."

"Yes, I suppose so," said Gustavus. "The trouble about the Shapeshifter is we don't know his real shape. Maybe it's that animal you saw."

"But why would he need to come to our house?" wondered Thomas.

"To see what you were like," said Caroline. "To see the lie of the land. Oh, gosh, maybe he's left a bugging device in the house. Maybe he'll be able to hear your every conversation."

"Then we'd better say nothing about this when we're at home," Gavin warned Thomas.

The thought of Samson Strange listening in on a bugging device for hours to Mother wittering on about celebrities and Father grunting made Thomas smile a little.

"I think, based on the evidence of the weird animal," said Gustavus, "that we can sort of assume Samson Strange is the Shapeshifter. Therefore, we'll have to burgle his house to see if the Wand is there. After all, he is the leader of the group who want to bring Demogorgon back."

"Oh, goody," said Thomas. "I love a good burgle."

"Hold on," protested Caroline. "First of all, we have to find out where he lives. Then, he's probably got the place burglar alarmed. What if he's there and surprises us?"

"He told us he lives near Petworth," said Gavin. "That's not far."

"We can ask in Petworth where he lives," suggested Caroline. "People will know, as he's a celebrated poet."

"Then we should go there and case the joint," said Gustavus.

In case you are unfamiliar with this quaint phrase, it means they would go there and have a preliminary look at the house to see the best way of burgling it.

"Burglar alarms won't be a problem," assured Gustavus. "I know a spell that will neutralise them easily. However, I do have a fear of magical guards."

"Do you mean sentries who weave spells?" asked Thomas.

"No," said Gustavus somberly, "I mean protective spells themselves."

"Even if we get in," interposed Gavin, "it will probably be in a safe or something. Can you break into safes, too, Wilkins?"

"One can but try," replied Gustavus, but he didn't sound quite so confident.

They went out and mounted their bicycles. Gavin groaned. He'd have to take Thomas on the crossbar again. It was four miles to Petworth.

****

We must now go back two months, before all these events took place. The Shapeshifter was sitting in his chamber and before him was a large mirror. Rather spookily, a voice spoke to him from the mirror.

"What would you now, Sorcerer?" it said.

"My schemes go well," said the Shapeshifter. "One thing I would know. Will any obstacle bar my way?"

"If you would succeed," said the voice in the mirror, "you must destroy the Tailors of Hillford. If you do not, they will be your doom."

There was only one family called Taylor in Hillford. The Shapeshifter discovered this through the Electoral Register. This was what had given him the idea to somehow arrange to visit them, with a view to working out the best way to destroy them. He found out Mother was a journalist and managed to get his agent to arrange an interview.

Chapter Nine

The town of Petworth in Sussex is not large. It boasts a population of less than three thousand. The cyclists were approaching it down the London Road, passing the Lower Pond on the right and then Hampers Green on the way into the town itself. The town features a stately home called Petworth House, which doesn't come into the story, nor do its gardens, designed by Lancelot Brown (known as Capability Brown) who was a whizzbang expert when it came to landscape gardening. The children paused in the centre of the town and asked some locals where they might find the home of the famous Samson Strange. The first person they questioned may have known, but, as he had a lisp and no teeth, they couldn't make out a word he said. The second was a lady of mature years, who was much more informative.

She told them it was in Grove Lane, outside the town limits. This could be reached by cycling down Grove Street, of which it formed a continuation. They resumed their cycling, Gavin complaining somewhat about the weight of Thomas.

"Poor Thomas, he's not heavy at all," sympathised Caroline. "Honestly, Gavin, you are a big wuss."

Before long they came to a house with a short driveway and this, they assumed, was the home of Samson Strange. The drive was unbarred by closed gates, so they wouldn't have to climb over any walls to get in.

The house itself had clearly been built by someone with money - and built quite recently, too. It looked very modern, even futuristic, with a door painted with black and white stripes like a zebra. I don't mean a zebra is painted with black and white stripes, they have them naturally. (Actually, a zebra is black with white stripes.) But the door was painted. Caroline felt it looked a bit tacky. The drive was gravelled and there was a gravelled patch outside the front door. The garden was quite large with a rockery and flower-bed. A bearded ancient was doing something mysterious in the flower bed with a trowel.

"Excuse me," said Gustavus, adopting his politest manner, "is this Mr Strange's house?"

"He ain't in," said the ancient horticulturist. "He's hout."

Caroline decided to use her feminine charms. Fluttering her eyelids she asked, "Can we have a look around? The gardens seem so beautiful."

The trowel plier replied without enthusiasm, "Round the back is better, but watch out for the dorg."

Leaving their bicycles at the front gates, the children walked, trying not to seem too purposeful, round to the back of the house.

The back garden was well laid out. If the house looked a little tasteless, the garden did not. There were bushes at regular intervals, a shrubbery and, towards the end, a fishpond. Suddenly, there was barking. This must have been the "dorg" of which they had been warned. It came rushing towards them, teeth first. It looked like a terrier of some sort, but none of the children knew of which breed. It was now they discovered what an advantage it was to have someone with mystical talents amongst them. Gustavus wove his hands in the air and the dog's eyes followed them, as though mesmerised. Then it lay down on the grass and fell into a sleep.

The children trooped up to the back of the house. "Look," said Gustavus, pointing to a wooden structure in the ground. "A way in. That'll lead to a coal cellar and I bet Mr Strange does not like to go out to bring his coal in, so there'll be a passage from there into the house."

They tried to lift this up, but found it was bolted from the inside.

"Can you magic bolts open?" asked Thomas hopefully.

"No," admitted Gustavus, "but I can do something else."

He took from his pocket what turned out to be a very powerful magnet. He held it against the wood and drew it to one side. As he did so, they heard the bolt slide back. The cellar door was now unlocked. It was the work of a second to open it.

"It's a coal cellar all right," said Gustavus, "but there's not much coal in it, as it's summer. And there is a passage leading into the house. That's how we'll get in."

They closed the door again.

"Only one thing remains," observed Caroline, "and that's to find the Wand when we get in."

At that moment a back door opened and a grouchy looking man in butler's apparel emerged. He took one look at the children and began to shout.

"Hey, you lot, get out of here. What do you think you're doing?"

"We're just admiring the gardens," said Caroline, trying to be charming again. The butler was impervious to charm.

"I'll have you arrested for trespassing if I catch you here again," he bellowed.

The children went, in a rather crestfallen fashion, around to the front. This butler certainly had put the kibosh on any hopes they might have had of getting into the building today. The gardener was still gardening.

"I yeard old Alvis giving you what for," he chuckled. "Not a nice fellow is Alvis. His mother came from Horsham, so I suppose it can't be helped."

Why mothers from Horsham tended to endow their offspring with bad tempers, the gardener did not say.

" 'E won't let me in the house, y'know," the gardener continued. "Every time I needs water, I has to go to the kitchen door and hand the bucket in and he or the cook woman fills it and hands it out. I walked in there once and got a right telling orf."

He lowered his voice.

"The floor felt hollow. I bet they've buried a dead body under it."

Chapter Ten

And so they returned to Hillford. They now, as I'm sure you've guessed, had deep suspicions that the Wand of Merlin might be hidden under the kitchen floor, but Gustavus had wisely pointed out that the hollow space beneath it might conceal something else unrelated to their concerns.

"Gosh, Thomas," said Gavin, "I think you've put on weight since we cycled here."

"Stop complaining, Beetle Brain," admonished Caroline. "You're always picking on Thomas."

I bet she and Gavin marry when they grow up, thought Gustavus. *She bosses him around like she was his wife.*

Gustavus had no real experience of family life and imagined from his rather wide reading that this was the normal state of affairs between married couples. Whether he was right, I leave to your own experience.

Gavin was feeling slightly glum. He it was who had discovered the secret of Gustavus Wilkins, yet the whole operation seemed to him to be getting dominated by Thomas, even though he was by far the youngest person there. Thomas brought out maternal instincts in Caroline and was, moreover, an assertive personality, whereas Gavin was more the quiet type. There was every likelihood he would grow up to be someone like Father, with an instinct to lie low (like Brer Rabbit) and say nuffin (like Brer Fox).

When they arrived back at the Wilkins ménage, they sat down for a Council of War. Gustavus, whatever his actual age, with all the instincts of a twelve-year old produced chocolate biscuits, fizzy orange (or soda, as Caroline insisted on calling it) and an invitation to the children to help themselves to anything else they wanted. Thomas spread marmite on his chocolate biscuits.

"Now I reckon," said Gustavus thoughtfully, "that the Wand is concealed in Samson Strange's house and that he is the Shapeshifter. It is also probable - but not certain - that it lies beneath the kitchen floor. However, someone like the Shapeshifter has probably got all sorts of secrets, so it may be that the kitchen hides something else entirely."

He paused to drink.

"We have to burgle that house some night and the sooner the better," he said.

"Well, that means tonight," said Gavin. "The longer we take about this, the greater the chances they will be able to free this Demogorgon."

"What do we know about this Princess?" wondered Caroline. "The one they're going to sacrifice. Have they got her yet?"

"I don't know," said Gustavus reflectively. "The only way we can recognise her is that she'll have a mark on her shoulder that is of a colour not known on earth."

"Won't she have long golden hair and be of surpassing beauty, like most Princesses in magical tales?" asked Thomas.

"This isn't a magical tale," said his brother sharply. "She may be as ugly as an old boot."

"Old boots aren't always ugly," said Thomas brightly. "Give some of them a polish and they look quite well. Do you remember Uncle Felix' old boots? They were----"

"I think we could look into the question of old boots later," said Gustavus. "I propose----"

"I accept," said Caroline wittily.

"Stop being a drongo," said Gavin.

A quarrel might have started, had not Thomas intervened by saying, "What is a *drongo* anyway? We all say it, but what does it mean?"

It was then Gustavus showed that he had lived longer than the others and knew more.

"It was the name of an Australian racehorse that lost all its races," he snapped. "Now let's get back to business. I suggest we meet tonight - say, just outside Hillford."

"There's that pub," said Gavin. "*The Chortling Horse.* It's easy to spot and we could meet up there."

"Say we meet about eleven," suggested Caroline. "I mean, we're all going to have to sneak out of our houses and that will take time."

"At least that means I don't have to pedal you up The Gripe," said Gavin to Thomas.

And so they returned to their various homes. Gavin was tired, what with his wakeful night and the morning's pedalling, so he lay down. He suggested Thomas also take a rest, as they would be faring forth at night. Thomas repaired to his bedroom, but he was so excited by the adventure that he was sure he wouldn't sleep. He was wrong. He did.

****

For those of you who don't know Sussex well, Worthing is a town on its south coast. There, at 5, Pring Avenue, lived George Featherstonehaugh. This is a long name, but it is pronounced Fanshaw, which is how I'm going to spell it. He was the President of the Worthing Cryptozoology Club, which investigated mystery animals. He telephoned Archibald Snodgrass, the club's only other member, in a state of some excitement.

"I say, Snodders, old bean," he began, "something absolutely spiffing has happened. I've had a call from a chap in Hillford. Said he saw a mystery animal in a neighbour's garden last night and asked us up there to investigate it. What thrills! I said we'd go up there tonight, see if the beastie reappears."

There was a gabbled answer from Archibald Snodgrass, to which Fanshaw replied, "I don't care if there's cricket on television tonight, you can watch the repeats. This bally well trumps cricket. See you at half past four. Yes, the usual place. Toodle-pip."

Chapter Eleven

Sneaking out after nightfall is an easy thing to do in books. Children do it all the time and then proceed to have dozens of adventures. It is not that easy in real life. For one thing, you have to wait until your parents are fully asleep. For Gavin and Thomas, once their parents were asleep getting out would be an easy business. Father slept like the Sleeping Beauty's twin brother and Mother, even if disturbed by noises at night, was immovable. The only trouble was that on that particular night, Mother and Father didn't go to bed. Father was watching the cricket on television live from Australia. Mother was writing up her article on a word processor that regularly stopped processing. It was certainly after eleven when the two of them ascended the stairs and it took an even longer time before Father's snores could be heard. Thomas left his bed and with infinite care tiptoed along the corridor that led to Gavin's room. Gavin, refreshed by the sleep he had had earlier, was dressed and ready. Gavin felt that Thomas was appropriately clad in a tracksuit, but didn't feel that the black mask he was wearing was entirely necessary. Thomas, on the other hand, felt it was *de rigeur* for every burglar to wear a black mask and could not be prevailed upon to remove his.

Gavin's bicycle lived in a shed in the back garden. The two boys made their way silently down the stairs and out of the back door. Just as they did so, the moon went behind a cloud, shrouding everything in utter darkness. That was why they didn't see the eager faces of Fanshaw and

Snodgrass looking over Mr Blackman's garden wall. They were not very well equipped. They had only a camera of the normal sort - nothing infa-red that might have penetrated the darkness or anything like that. But Fanshaw saw well in the dark and suddenly discerned that there was something moving next door.

"Over there," he whispered.

"What?" said Snodgrass in a loud voice, forgetting the need for stealth.

"There's somebody over there," whispered Gavin. "I heard a voice."

"So did I," whispered Thomas. "I bet it's the Shapeshifter or his minions."

"Look," said Gavin. "Someone's climbing over the wall."

Thomas picked up a flower pot. "Let's see how he likes this," he murmured.

The flowerpot flew through the air, catching Snodgrass in mid-clamber.

"Egad, it's got me," he cried, falling backwards, all efforts at silence now abandoned.

Fanshaw, who had a torch, shone it on his friend and saw he had been hit with a flowerpot. He then sent a beam of his torch over the fence and for just a minute made out masked Thomas's face as the two boys raced for the cover of the shed. Fanshaw then turned to his companion and noticed that he was bleeding. He helped him to his feet and the two of them struggled to Mr Blackman's back door, which the latter was just inside. He had been monitoring the cryptozoologists' progress.

"What happened?" he asked aghast, looking at the blood flowing from Snodgrass' forehead over his ashen face.

"I've discovered your mystery animal, Mr Blackman," he said. "It's a raccoon. I saw the mask raccoons have around their eyes when I shone the bally torch on him. Perhaps it escaped from a fur farm."

"The animal I saw wasn't a raccoon," began Mr Blackman.

"Do you know what a raccoon is?" asked Fanshaw. "It's an American animal-----"

"Of course I know what a festering raccoon is and it wasn't what I saw last night," retorted Mr Blackman. "Do you think I'd have called you out if I'd only seen a snerfing raccoon?"

"I'm dying," said Snodgrass clutching his head.

"Well, go and die somewhere else," said Mr Blackman. "The pair of you are clearly utterly incompetent. The front door's that way."

A somewhat crestfallen Fanshaw, helping his comrade, struggled out to their car. They got in.

"I'm going to be sick," said Snodgrass and was.

"You could have done that before we got into the car," rebuked

Fanshaw, whose car it was. "Looks to me like you've dashed well got concussion. I'll take you to A & E."

When all the noise died down, Gavin and Thomas emerged from the shed. Gavin mounted his bicycle and Thomas climbed onto the crossbar. They had already telephoned Gustavus to say they would be a little late in arriving.

****

Gavin and Thomas had not been the only ones to experience difficulties in quitting their homes that night. In Caroline's house, Aunt Thelma had come to visit.

Aunt Thelma, like many an enthusiastic American before her, was visiting England to see all the sights. She wasn't really Caroline's aunt, she was her father's, but she refused to be called Great Aunt Thelma.

"It would just *kill* me to be addressed as a great aunt," she had protested. "It would make me feel as though I had one foot in the grave."

She was, in fact, a lively creature who rather embarrassed Mr Zuppinger (Caroline's father). The latter was a brusque, efficient businessman who *got things done*. He had little time to waste on his fellow human beings unless the making of money was involved. He was employed by some transatlantic technology firm and had no life outside it, except for the occasional game of golf, in which he partook, not to gain enjoyment, but to obtain clients. Caroline's mother, Mrs Zuppinger, had some sort of job, I forget what exactly, but her husband considered it was vastly less important than his, as it brought in less money. On this particular night, both of them and Caroline were held captive by Aunt Thelma, who insisted on showing them shots of the sites she had visited.

"Look," she said, "there's the shot I took of Buckingham Palace, except you can't see it so well because that truck drove in front of it just as I was taking the picture."

And there were many more like that.

Caroline at length pleaded fatigue and headed for her bedroom, but there was no way her parents or her great aunt were calling a halt to the evening. It finally dawned on her that she would have to get out while her parents were still up.

She knew how to do this, for she had read about it in books. She took the sheets from her bed and knotted them into a rope. Luckily, the bed was near the window. She tied one end of her makeshift rope to the leg of the bed. Then she opened her window and prepared to lower herself down into what she termed the backyard.

In books, these ropes of sheets always stay firmly knotted together. Caroline was to discover that this was not necessarily true in real life. When she had clambered down the rope for quite a short time, it came apart and she plummeted to the ground. She might have been quite badly hurt if she hadn't fallen into the pile of manure her mother was planning to use on the flower bed. It was nice, squishy, soft manure so Caroline was hardly hurt at all.

At about half-past one the *Chortling Horse* was long closed and there were no grown-ups about when Gavin and Thomas finally turned up. Gustavus and Caroline were already there, but for some reason Gustavus was keeping well back from Caroline.

Chapter Twelve

The quartet of would-be burglars made their way to Samson Strange's house.

"Should we cut the telephone lines, so they cannot call for help?" suggested Thomas, remembering a burglary in a book he had once read.

"My dear Thomas," said Gustavus, "we are in the age of the mobile phone. Such stratagems are out of date. Oh, curses, the gates are closed."

Yes, while Samson Strange's gateway had been unbarred by gates in the daytime, its gates were shut and locked by night.

"Have you any gate-opening spells?" wondered Caroline hopefully.

"No," said Gustavus shortly.

"Skeleton keys, perhaps?" suggested Thomas.

"No," said Gustavus, even more shortly. Actually, it's really impossible to say one *no* more shortly than another, but it sounded as if he'd said it more shortly.

"Then," said Gavin, "it's lucky that, as well as Fatty Thomas, I brought something else on the back of my bike."

He removed a leather bag from the carrier of his bike.

"This," he said, "contains Father's acetylene torch and protective goggles."

"Gavin," said Gustavus, "you are a genius. You must have anticipated locked doors. There I was thinking you were nothing more than Thomas's pudding-like brother, almost a non-person, and it was you who foresaw this problem."

"It's nice to know you had such a high opinion of me, Wilkins," said Gavin. Clearly, if Gustavus had learned anything from being twenty-two, it hadn't been tact. Gavin donned the goggles and turned on the torch, melting the lock quickly. Our heroes opened the gates and entered.

They went across the grass, so their feet wouldn't crunch on the gravel, and around by the side of the house. The moonlight was good enough to light their way.

There were no lights showing from Samson Strange's house, either front or back. To use Thomas's phrase, it was "shrouded in darkness". Hopefully, all its denizens were asleep.

Then the "dorg" started to bark inside the house. Gustavus made some mystic gestures in the air. "It should be asleep now," he breathed. Certainly, there was no more barking.

They reached the cellar door and Gustavus produced his mega-magnet. Slowly and almost silently, but not so silently that they couldn't hear it, the bolt slid back. They raised up the door and slid down into the murky depths beneath.

"I've brought a flashlight," whispered Caroline, shining it around the chamber.

They heard a scuttling sound. A fleeing rodent, no doubt. Gavin had always had a fear of rats and mice, even when they were going in the opposite direction. And, if there was one down here, were there more? His imagination conjured up huge furry rats with broken yellow fangs and an attitude problem.

Gustavus had also brought a torch and shone it about. They soon discovered the passage leading from cellar to house and had started to go up it when Gustavus suddenly hissed, "Stop!"

Everyone did so. They didn't know what Gustavus had seen, but imagined all sorts of horrors. Caroline in particular imagined snakes. Did Samson Strange keep the odd cobra in the passage to deter unwelcome visitors? However, what Gustavus had seen was no cobra, but an electric eye.

In case you're not a burglar-alarm expert, let me explain to you what this is. A small round device is placed in the wall. It sends an invisible beam out to another device at the other side. If you step through the invisible beam, it sets off the alarm.

The electric eye was near the ground. Gustavus pointed it out to the others in whispered tones. Each stepped carefully over the beam. Then they proceeded to the passage door and opened it. It opened into a long passage way. As this was carpeted and its one window curtained, they reckoned they had come into the main body of the house.

"Now to find the kitchen," said Gustavus.

They were at the back of the house, so they assumed the kitchen wouldn't be too far away. They opened a door that led into a small scullery. This in turn led into the kitchen.

The kitchen was not unusual as kitchens go. The floor was tiled.

"Now to start digging," said Gustavus.

He produced a levering tool, with which he tried to lever up the tiles.

"You'll have to cut through the glue holding them down," said Caroline helpfully.

Happily Gustavus had thought of this and produced a knife of the kind favoured by the Swiss Army.

It was then that they heard footsteps descending a flight of stairs.

Chapter Thirteen

If you are performing a burglary, there is nothing that is more alarming than the sound of approaching feet. I expect you know that, even if you've never burgled anywhere, but nonetheless you really have to have undergone this experience to appreciate how terrifying it is. Gavin's stomach seemed to do a somersault and I'm sure most of the others reacted in much the same way, but Caroline kept her cool enough to hiss, "Back into the scullery."

They did as bidden. Happily, Gustavus' knife hadn't really damaged the floor yet. Samson Strange walked in. He was humming a little hum, a tune famous in times gone by called *Old Man Mose*. He was also procuring something from the fridge. Then they heard Alvis, the butler, approaching.

"Sorry, sir," said Alvis. "I couldn't sleep. I came down to make myself a cup of tea."

"Help yourself," said Samson Strange. "By the way, I much admire your dressing-gown. Is that a Chinese dragon on the back of it?"

They continued exchanging pleasantries for a few minutes and then Samson the poet said, "Don't come into the dining room tonight, Alvis. I have to create a wormhole to bring here someone who dwells in a far-off land."

"Very well, sir," said Alvis.

Alvis was obviously privy in some degree to Samson Strange's magical operations.

They finished their cups of tea. (Alvis had made one for Samson Strange as well as himself). Then they departed and our little gang of housebreakers emerged from the scullery.

"Gavin, you continue with the digging," instructed Gustavus, handing him the knife. "I want to see what Samson is doing."

One of the first things Gustavus had insisted on learning when apprenticed to Professor Vilnius had been the secret of becoming invisible. This is actually quite a hard exercise if you want to use natural magic, it consists largely in deflecting light coming in your direction. But Gustavus had mastered it and now he began to disappear from sight as he followed Samson Strange. They reached the door of the dining room and entered, Samson Strange in front, thoughtfully swinging the door shut so it hit Gustavus behind him. Gustavus only just managed to enter the room before Samson Strange turned around and closed the door properly.

The dining room contained a long table which the Shapeshifter moved to one side, apparently by some sort of kinetic energy. Then he concentrated hard and Gustavus could actually feel the waves of concentration being projected from his mind, even though they were not being projected in his direction. Eventually in the dark a kind of tunnel began to form, its entrance looking a little like a gigantic smoke ring. After some time the Shapeshifter stopped, panting from his exertions. Then down the hole towards him came what Gustavus at first thought was a beautiful lady.

She had lengthy black hair, but her face was so white it looked as though it were a mask formed of some artificial whiteness. It looked more like putty than flesh. Her mouth seemed as though it were covered by a garishly red lipstick, but Gustavus realised this was its natural colour. Her nails were long and red as her mouth and she gave the Shapeshifter a sneering smile, showing pointed teeth, teeth that looked as if they had been especially filed. They weren't the long teeth of a vampire, but there was no stumpishness about them. She wore, not a dress, but a suit of light golden armour, which Gustavus knew to be made of a well-nigh impenetrable metal found on some distant meteor.

"Greetings, Lilith," boomed Samson Strange.

"Greetings to thee, Shapeshifter," responded Lilith. "What ails thee that thou needst my help, O being who glorieth in his own power?"

"Lilith, dost thou know we shall soon release the Old One, the Tentacled One, from his place of durance. Knowest thou that, having freedom, I will loom high in his counsels and his trust when he is lord of the earth?"

Lilith laughed. "What, thou wouldst release Demogorgon? Thou art a fool, Shapeshifter. With Demogorgon ever his friend today was his foe tomorrow. You may stand at his side proudly as his henchman at the start, but soon he will destroy thee, as he hath destroyed many another."

"Lilith," responded Samson Strange, "this do I know all too well. Therefore, here is my plan. When he is freed and has enslaved the earth, thou and I shall unite and take his dominion from him. Singly we cannot. Ever since he was placed in that rocky crevice, his power hath grown like a spreading fungus. But together our powers are greater than his. We can cut him down like an oak tree and take the lordship of earth for ourselves. Think, o murtherer of infants, of the prey that will make ready for thy thirsting jaws."

Gustavus knew what he meant. Lilith was a demoness, who went about killing babies. She had, in elder times, been regarded with horror. Although not a vampire in the strict sense, yet she sucked the blood of her victims.

Said Lilith, "I shall return to my haunts by the Incarnadined Waters that sunder Egypt from Araby. To thy words I shall give my consideration. I will come again and give thee my answer."

She retreated back into the wormhole, going backwards so her eyes were always on the Shapeshifter, until at last the wormhole closed and darkness only was in its place. Walking exhaustedly, Samson Strange left the room. A few minutes later Gustavus left behind him.

****

While all this was taking place, the other children had been digging up the floor in the kitchen. Under the tiles they found floorboards, but these were easily removed. Beneath them they found a casket, fashioned of orichalc. I cannot describe orichalc, never having seen it. Slowly they opened it, to discover inside what looked at first glance like a tube, but on further investigation, proved to be a thick wand. Caroline touched it, then gave a quick yelp, as though she had received an electric shock, and fastened the lid. At that moment Gustavus appeared. I don't mean he turned visible again - he had done that already - but he came through the door.

"Well done," he congratulated.

But Caroline's yelp had been heard. It had been heard by the "dorg", which started to yap. But it had also been heard by Samson Strange the Shapeshifter, who came running towards the kitchen.

Chapter Fourteen

As Samson Strange ran towards the kitchen, the children ran into the scullery and down the passage towards the cellar. In the dark they did not hesitate, even when they set off the electric eye in the passage (having forgotten it was there), and they yanked themselves up out of the cellar entrance. Gustavus helped Thomas with this, as he was too small to reach the opening. Then they ran around the house to the front gate, where their bicycles were waiting. Gustavus put Thomas on his crossbar, as he reckoned Gavin would be too tired to cycle quickly.

The electric eye had set off the alarm in the house and it was a sharp and piercing alarm, designed to penetrate the most deeply sleeping brain. Alvis woke up and picked up the nearest blunt instrument he could find - a croquet mallet that had somehow found its way into his bedroom. Samson Strange was busy transforming himself into the appalling beast seen a couple of nights before.

You might think that, if you were a were-beast or something similar, you just changed into one - poof! - like that. However, it takes somewhat longer. You see, it isn't just your outside that changes into a beast, your insides have to do so as well, changing their shape, elongating, shortening, stretching. I imagine it is not all that comfortable. Just as the transformation was complete, Alvis came around the corner.

While Alvis clearly knew Samson Strange had some sorcerous powers, he obviously hadn't known about the shape shifting ones. He saw the appalling creature, neither canine nor feline, not to be found in any manual of zoology, with diseased fur and a grotesque bejowled face, covered in suppurating pustules which exuded green liquid matter and with huge, yellow-brown teeth facing him. Alvis did not attack this creature with his croquet mallet. He fainted. The scent of his prone body excited the Shapeshifter's hunger, but he had no time to devour Alvis now. His animal instincts were to the fore. He bounded towards the cellar and into the back garden.

For some reason it did not occur to the Shapeshifter that the children would have run around to the front. He assumed that, as they had run into the back garden, they would have overleaped the garden wall, which led into Horrocks' Farm, which adjoined his property. With a bound he leaped over the wall himself.

Farmer Horrocks had been awoken by the sound of the alarm next door. He had dragged himself from his bed to see what was going on. He saw, in the field behind the farmhouse, a beast which beggared imagination, a beast that looked like something prehistoric, indeed, a beast that looked too horrible to be prehistoric. He looked on transfixed as it sniffed the air and ground, trying to pick up the children's scent. It then went bounding off. Farmer Horrocks ran down the stairs and rang up the local constabulary.

The Shapeshifter had picked up a human scent. Unfortunately for him, it was the wrong human scent. It was that of Dennis Tomlinson, poacher. Dennis Tomlinson made his progress by hidden ways in the countryside. He had been planning to shoot a deer on a nearby deer farm and take it home. Suddenly he was aware of something pacing through the undergrowth behind him. He turned around swiftly and aimed his gun, though he thought it would be nothing more than a badger. It wasn't a badger. The Shapeshifter in his horrific guise was approaching. Dennis Tomlinson aimed his gun, fired, missed and ran. The Shapeshifter, seeing this was not his quarry, turned, snarled and moved off in the other direction. When Dennis Tomlinson reached the roadside he passed out. There he was found by Amos Farrington, postman, next morning, and taken to hospital.

Meanwhile, the children had had an exhausting ride home. Gustavus had taken a turnoff for Tandem Road and the others reached Gavin's house.

"We can get in, because we left the back door unlocked," whispered Gavin. "How are you going to get in?" he asked Caroline.

"Oh, I can sneak in by the cat flap," she replied. "See you guys in the morning."

Gavin and Thomas, the former carrying the orichalc casket which contained the Wand of Merlin, made their way into their house.

Chapter Fifteen

The next day was an active one. It began with the arrival of the fire engine, whose firefighters had the task of getting Caroline out of the cat flap, in which she had stuck. Gavin's Mother gazed through her lace-curtained window, trying to make out what was going on.

"Harold, there's a fire engine next door," she said. "Do you think they've had a fire?"

"Uh!" responded Father, showing deep feelings of uninterest.

"Harold, do come out of that newspaper and pay attention," Mother rasped at him.

Father suddenly looked up. "Where are the children?" he wondered.

This was a long sentence for father at breakfast and even the dog looked startled.

"They seem to be dead tired, so I thought I'd let them sleep in," Mother replied. "Never mind about the children, Harold. What's going on next door?"

"Something that's none of our business," said Father, taking a sip of tea. "If there are firemen there, they'll be able to handle whatever it is."

He rarely read out bits from the paper, but, for once, he was in a slightly talkative mood.

"It says here there was the sighting of a mysterious beast near Petworth last night," he told her. "Apparently in the moonlight you could look through its skin and see all its innards. Heart, liver, lungs, intestines------"

"Stop being disgusting, Harold, and get on with your breakfast," chided Mother.

Thus chidden, Father uttered no more. A curtain of silence descended on the breakfast table.

Next door, Caroline was in deep, deep trouble. She had been found, dressed but asleep, in the cat flap where she had wedged herself trying to get in the night before. Mr Zuppinger had no time to deal with the fact that his daughter had seemingly made a nocturnal excursion. He had to meet a Mr Naismith who, like himself, was a totally uninteresting man whose whole mind was given over to business. "You deal with it, Darlene," he told his wife. "I have to get up to London."

When he had left the house, Darlene Zuppinger turned her penetrating gaze to her daughter.

"What were you doing outside?" she demanded and her eyes seemed to bore into a very sleepy Caroline's brain like gimlets.

What Caroline would have answered I certainly don't know and I don't think Caroline knew either, but at that moment Mrs Zuppinger's attention was mercifully distracted by Aunt Thelma's falling down the stairs.

It wasn't that she landed merely with a crash at the foot of the stairs. She crashed against every step on the way down, while bits of her banged against the wall and the balustrade. Indeed, Mrs Zuppinger was rather surprised that some bits of her hadn't come off in the fall. Mrs Zuppinger, examining her, decided she had a possibly broken wrist and ankle, various contusions, a bruise on her forehead and a vocabulary of bad language which she never had suspected lay in her field of knowledge; for Aunt Thelma was not knocked out. Aunt Thelma was swearing like a crowd of pirates who had discovered someone had stolen their rum. Mrs Zuppinger, with the aid of Caroline, half-carried her bulky form over to the car. That's Aunt Thelma's bulky form, not Mrs Zuppinger's. Mrs Zuppinger's figure was what might be described as "trim": her husband insisted upon it, so she looked well whenever they had to attend a business function as a couple.

"I'll be having words with you, young lady," she said threateningly, as she clambered into the driver's seat.

Caroline had no doubt she spoke truly.

****

"I say, Snodders, old bean."

George Fanshaw's voice was sparkling with enthusiasm as he rang his colleague.

"Have you seen the paper? They've spotted a mystery beast outside Petworth. We must investigate at once."

"I do not wish to hunt monsters any more," came the voice of Archibald Snodgrass. "I am resigning from the Worthing Cryptozoology Club."

"You can't do that," Fanshaw protested, horror in his voice. "This could make our name. Put us on the map."

"I do not wish to be put on any map," replied Snodgrass. "I wish to be left in peace. They kept me in A & E overnight for observation. This meant that a muscle-bound nurse with a tattooed arm and a moustache kept asking me if I wanted to throw up again."

"Well, they employ a lot of male nurses these days," Fanshaw pointed out.

"It wasn't a male nurse," Snodgrass replied. "It was female, but whether it was female human or female wart-hog I couldn't quite decide. I am not going into work today. I need complete rest."

And with that he hung up.

Fanshaw was crestfallen. Like Cain in the Bible, his countenance fell. But a surprise was in store for him. This came in the form of a knock on the door. It was Myrtle Singleton, reporter from the *Petworth Clarion.* Miss Singleton was full of youthful enthusiasm.

"Mr Featherstonehaugh?" she enquired.

"Yes, but I pronounce it Fanshaw," explained Fanshaw. He had spent half his life explaining to people how to pronounce his name.

"I'm Myrtle Singleton from the *Petworth Clarion.* I believe that you're a Coprozoologist. I've been sent to interview you about our recently seen monster. Then I thought we might go and have a look at the places where it was seen."

George Fanshaw was much taken by the good looks and bubbling effervescence of his interlocutor.

"What a spiffing idea," he said. "We could look for tracks and droppings."

"I'll do the tracks and you can do the droppings," said Myrtle. "Can you come right away, Mr Fanshott?"

"It's Fanshaw," he replied, "but you can call me George."

****

In two different parts of Hillford General Hospital, two different conversations of note were taking place. One was in A & E, where Aunt Thelma was being seen promptly to get her out of the waiting room, where her language had been making the vegetation wilt. She had insisted that Mrs Zuppinger stay with her, much as the latter would have liked to distance herself from both aunt and language. In another part of the hospital Gustavus, Caroline, Gavin and Thomas were looking at the very unwell form of Professor Vilnius.

It is true that Professor Vilnius was a little better this morning. The doctors would tell him nothing about his condition, mainly because they didn't know anything about his condition. They knew it hadn't been a heart attack. Beyond that they could not go. They were conducting further tests.

"That generally means they come and stick needles in me," he complained. Having needles stuck in him was clearly not to his taste.

Gustavus told him about the peculiar interview he had witnessed between the Shapeshifter and the almost vampiric woman called Lilith. He hadn't told the other children about this either, due to lack of time. The name Lilith meant nothing to any of the children, but it certainly meant something to Professor Vilnius.

"*Lilith!*" he exclaimed. "She is a feared demoness who seeks to kill as many babies as possible. Jewish legend said she was the first wife of Adam, but she abandoned him, If she and the Shapeshifter were to combine their powers and use the Wand of Merlin, nothing could stand in their way. Their power would be far greater even than Demogorgon's. Their union would be a catastrophe."

He stopped to splutter. He felt that what he had to say merited a splutter.

"There is only one thing for it," he said. "You must take the Wand to Logres. There they will know what steps to take."

"Where's Logres," asked Caroline.

"Hang on," said Gavin, "I've heard of Logres. It was the name of England when King Arthur ruled it."

"True," said the Prof. "After the Romans left Britain, the country split into several states. Then the Angles, Saxons and Jutes started attacking it. Arthur united the Britons against them. He was victorious, but, after the disastrous battle of Camlann, the Angles and Saxons took over, nor must we forget the Jutes, who were in the Isle of Wight. That's why we speak English today. The Ancient Britons became the ancestors of the Welsh and Cornish.

"However, Arthur had a son to succeed him. His name was Gwydre. He isn't mentioned much in Arthurian stories you read, but he is remembered in Welsh tradition, which says that he was killed by the Boar-God Twrch Trwyth, but you can't believe everything legend tells you. In the depths of the woods of Hampshire he established small a secret territory which exists to this very day. Magic keeps outsiders from finding it. The present ruler is King Lamorak. They are awaiting the time when their dynasty can reclaim Britain once more. They call their little land Logres. However, there they will know the best way to protect the Wand of Merlin; and, without the Wand of Merlin, the plans of Demogorgon and the Shapeshifter and Lilith will never succeed."

"Professor Vilnius is very ill and I think he's talked enough," said a rather officious looking nurse with a clipboard. "I think you should leave him alone now."

"Instructions for getting to Logres are in the safe in my private room," said the Prof. "Mrs Jarvis will show you how to open it."

"Now, run along children," said the nurse, her tone of command growing more menacing. A touch of menace in your voice is a handy thing to have if you want to be a nurse.

The children departed the hospital and mercifully didn't run into Mrs Zuppinger, as they would have done had they departed a few minutes earlier.

Chapter Sixteen

The children returned to Gustavus' house. They had been discussing on the way back how to get to the hidden settlement of Logres, ruled by the lineal descendant of King Arthur. The trouble was it was situated in the New Forest.

The New Forest is in the west of Hampshire and spreads into adjoining counties. It is not by any means new, having been planted in the 11th Century, but it was new when they first planted it and that's how it got its name. The trouble was that they would have to go first to Pulborough to obtain details of how to get to the secret settlement from Katy Jarvis, then take bus or train into Hampshire (the next county) and then find their way to the New Forest. This was going to be a long and tortuous journey, dependent as they were on public transport, and if they had to take a train to Southampton (a possibility) they doubted if they had enough money for the fares.

"What a pity Gustavus doesn't look his age," sighed Caroline. "Then we could hire a car."

"Hang on," said Gavin, "I know how to drive a car. My Uncle Roger taught me. If Gustavus' magic could make me look like an adult, then we could get one and drive it."

"Well, it can't," said Gustavus. "I'm only an *apprentice* magician. But we could disguise Gavin as a grown-up."

"We'd never get away with it," said Caroline. "He's not tall enough."

"I think I have a solution," piped up Thomas.

Every face swivelled in his direction. They had come to the realisation that, whenever a solution was required, Thomas, despite his tender years, was the one to turn to.

"We put Gavin in the front seat, sitting on cushions so he looks taller. Then we make up his face to look old - that shouldn't be too difficult - and give him a false beard. He could fool any onlooker who sees him driving."

"That's a good idea," agreed Gavin. "But when I walk into the car hire place, they'll spot my height."

"In that case we'll have to just pinch a car," said Thomas. "As the fate of the world is at stake, it won't really be stealing. It's a matter of necessity."

"Maybe we could make Caroline up too and she could sit next to Gavin and pretend to be his wife," suggested Gustavus archly.

"Maybe we couldn't," said Caroline firmly. "I have standards."

Well, to cut a long story short - and what else would you do with a long story? - they made Gavin up remarkably well. They nearly overdid it and made him look a bit too geriatric, with white hair and many wrinkles. (Gustavus had had a box of theatrical makeup in his house).

"You look older that Aunt Thelma," laughed Caroline.

Now it was time to purloin a car.

They quitted the house and looked up and down the road for cars parked on it. However, most of Tandem Road's cars had been driven by their owners to work. The only available car was Mr Gascoigne's. That, unfortunately, looked as if it had seen better days.

They went along and had a look at it. Rust, they saw, provided varying colour to parts of the outside. Other parts had what could be called an unkempt look if you could use the word in connection with cars. The wheels looked as if they resented attachment to the main body of the vehicle. How this thing had ever passed an MOT, the children could not imagine. With a piece of wire Gustavus opened the door. Gavin and Caroline climbed into the front, Gustavus and Thomas went into the back. Gavin's Uncle Roger, apart from showing him how to drive a car, had shown him how to start one by hotwiring it. Let us say Uncle Roger had had a chequered past.

"What kind of car is this anyway?" asked Caroline. "I've never seen anything quite like it."

"It's a Csardas," said the knowledgeable Gustavus. "They make them in the east of Europe. Haven't you seen the advertisement for them on TV - Functional but Fast?"

The engine started. Some car engines, when they start, can be referred to as *purring*. This one might better be described as *wheezing*. Slowly it moved into the centre of the road, then down the left side.

Truth to tell, when Uncle Roger had taught Gavin to drive, he hadn't taught him very thoroughly. He had given him a few perfunctory lessons in a field, where they had nearly hit a cow. Moreover, the controls of Uncle Roger's car had been somewhat different from those of a Csardas. But Gavin could recognise some of them, such as the steering wheel.

With a cough from the engine the vehicle set off down the road. Mr Gascoigne's cat Tiddles watched the proceedings with a marked lack of interest. Mr Gascoigne, in the house, was watching a television programme called *Learn Punjabi,* because he had always wanted to learn Punjabi. He did not hear his vehicle's departure.

The main road to Pulborough was not much troubled by traffic, I am pleased to say, but any car behind the Csardas passed it swiftly by. It may have been Functional but it was scarcely Fast, whatever the TV advertisements might have had to say of its prowess. Not alone did it creep along, but any motorist coming behind was enveloped in large clouds of smoke which emerged from the exhaust.

"I'm feeling sick," warned Thomas ominously, but fortunately the contents of his stomach lingered in their place of repose.

"Who designed this thing?" wondered Caroline.

Two cyclists going in the opposite direction espied it.

"That's a Csardas," explained one. "You don't see many of them about. Can't think why."

The mercy of the matter was that the Csardas, unable to go at more than twenty miles an hour, posed no danger to other vehicles, despite the driver's inexperience, and it was not long before Pulborough drew into sight.

The dwelling of Professor Vilnius was on Mare Hill Road and thither our travellers repaired. Caroline was solicitous for Thomas, but the latter said he was feeling much better now. She was fairly scathing as regards the driving skills of Gavin. Gavin merely snorted back at her. Snorting is a rather indecorous thing to do. Manuals of etiquette frown on it. Gavin, however, had never read a manual of etiquette. It was then they saw a policeman up ahead, signalling them to stop.

This was Constable Gashforth, a man who knew his way about. Although he couldn't make out the driver of the car clearly, he could see there was something odd about his features. In the police, if you see something odd, you investigate. Gavin applied the brakes and the car drew to a halt.

Constable Gashforth, on looking in, couldn't decide whether the driver was a dwarf or a disguised juvenile. He tapped on the window, which Gavin lowered.

"May I see your driving licence, sir?" he said, not noticing that Gustavus, in the back seat, was making arcane gestures with his hands.

Suddenly Gashforth felt dizzy. It was as if he had developed pins and needles in his brain. He staggered backward and fell into a ditch at the roadside. There he entered into a deep sleep. He dreamed for a moment he was in a sandy desert, pursuing an ostrich that had gone through a red light, and then his sleep became deeper and he dreamt no more. He also forgot completely about the car. A slight but distinct snore proceeded from his nose. Our carload of heroes went on to the residence of Professor Vilnius.

They were greeted there by Katy, who was waiting for them, as the Professor had somehow got word to her from the hospital. She told Gavin in no uncertain terms that his disguise as an old man was ineffective.

"Go and wash that muck off your face," she told him. "I'll drive you as far as the New Forest. After that, follow the instructions on this map."

The map she showed him was hand drawn, with instructions written in Dr Vilnius' rather antiquated hand, but Gustavus could read them. Gavin scrubbed his face while Thomas looked on and gave critical advice. His skin felt quite sore when he was at last clean.

"It took you long enough," grumbled Caroline.

"He's got an unsightly rash on his cheek," supplied Thomas.

"You'll have an unsightly black eye in a minute," growled Gavin.

"You can't hit poor Thomas, he has glasses," pointed out the protective Caroline.

"In a minute he'll have bruises to go with them," snarled Gavin.

"Now, you children mustn't fight," observed Katy. "Little birds in the nests who fight fall out and get eaten by foxes."

She herded them into her car, which I'm happy to say was not a Csardas, and they set off.

"There's that pore policeman you told me about, still asleep in his ditch," remarked Katy as they passed the snoozing form of Constable Gashforth.

The drive to the New Forest was uneventful. It was certainly less tense, as the children were not fearing being stopped at any moment by some inquisitive officer of the law. When they reached the borders of the treed expanse, they bade farewell to Katy and made their way into the forest. Gustavus was elected map reader, as he could best understand the Professor's unique hand and before long they found themselves on a little path or track way, bordered on each side by sturdy trees.

They saw in the distance a stockade, a wooden fence. Had you or I been in the forest, we would not have made it out, as magical methods concealed it from most wayfarers. But Gustavus and his party were not wayfarers. Gavin was beginning to feel that this was quite an exciting adventure to get into, when an arrow struck the tree in front of him.

Chapter Seventeen

"Run!" bellowed Gustavus and, despite his girth, he began to do this at an enviable pace. Caroline, realising that Thomas would not be able to run as quickly as the others, grabbed his wrist and pulled him along. Gavin looked briefly to one side, but did not slow his pace as he pelted forwards. Arrows were being shot at them by ugly little men, three to four feet high, with red caps on their heads.

They look like Goblins, he thought and I can confirm that Goblins is indeed what they were. These creatures roved the inner recesses of the New Forest and were the servants of the Shapeshifter, who had long known of the secret settlement of Logres. Their assignment was to eliminate anyone trying to get into it. Their archery skills weren't particularly good and, at that moment, there issued from the stockade a bunch of Dwarfs, also armed with bow and arrow, who let fly at the Goblins. I don't know how many they hit, as the inside of a forest, with all those trees, makes archery quite difficult. Gavin saw one Goblin drop his bow when he was struck in the hand. But the Goblins, it seemed, didn't feel like a full scale fight. At the sight of the Dwarfs, they turned and fled.

The leading Dwarf, who had a slightly superior look about him, appeared and bowed.

"Master Gustavus," he said, "it is some years since last we

saw you in these parts. The Professor sent word that you were coming. On King Lamorak's behalf, I greet you."

He led them into the palisaded village, which Gavin noted contained about thirty cottages with thatched roofs and an open building he took to be a forge, as it had an anvil inside it, but it was not in use at the moment. A large log cabin proved to be King Lamorak's palace, though it was much too small to be a real palace. The door was opened by a Dwarf and it led them directly into a long hall, which contained a circular table at which King Lamorak sat.

King Lamorak was black. Well, not entirely black. He was of mixed race. He was also the only human in the room. The others there were Dwarfs or, in some cases, smaller but similar beings, whom our heroes were later to discover were Gnomes. Even smaller was a little round humanoid sitting near the hearth. This was the household Hob. A Hob, I should tell you, was a creature who protected the building.

King Lamorak's voice was loud and sonorous. Even when sitting, he looked very tall. A crown encircled his head.

"Come in and be welcome, travellers," he invited. "The Professor's warning of your arrival has reached us."

Gavin wondered how exactly it had reached them. Did they have mobile phones in this medieval looking place? Perhaps he used telepathy, though when last they had seen him he didn't look up to vigorous mental activity.

"Be seated, be seated," said the King, indicating wooden chairs about his table. "I gather you do not know much about our little kingdom. Let me enlighten you. We were established here after the unhappy fall of my ancestor King Arthur at the Battle of Camlann. Melian the wizard ensorcelled the place so no passers-by could see it, but it transpired that other dwellers in the wood could do so. Each of us has had to marry a princess of royal lineage to keep the place intact. It is, however, hard to find folk of royal descent when one is hid in the woods. My mother was a princess of the Ethiopian royal family, descended from Menelik, son of King Solomon."

"Have you found any princess yet?" asked Caroline, who was finding all this quite interesting.

"I am not yet wed," returned the King, "but my envoys are on their way to the secret city of Gran Paititi, concealed in the jungles of South America. It is a city established by Tupac Amaru the Second, last of the Incas, where his line still rules. They are hoping to negotiate a marriage with a princess there" Suddenly he clapped his hands. "Bring food and drink for my guests!" he boomed and it was brought with much scuttling.

Dwarfs brought plates of food to the table. Gavin looked suspiciously at it, as it resembled nothing he had seen before, except possibly large fishcakes. It did not, however, look like buns baked in an oven. He took an exploratory bite. He hoped it didn't taste of fish. He couldn't abide fish. But he was happy to discover it had a pleasant taste, though one he couldn't readily describe. It didn't taste *like* anything. Thomas had already started eating. The food came in the form of circular baps and you had a knife to cut it with, but no forks appeared. Thomas, who would eat just about anything, was already wolfing his way into his portion. They were also served with a sparkling fruit-flavoured drink which came in pottery goblets. Although they didn't think so at the time, Gavin was to realise later that they had actually dined with a king.

When they could eat no more, the King cleared his throat a little and said, "I believe you have brought me a gift."

Gustavus took from his rucksack the casket containing the Wand of Merlin, the King opened it and called on a Dwarf, who took it to, Gavin assumed, some secure location.

"I think now," said the King, "we need no longer worry about Demogorgon and the Shapeshifter. The powers left to them are insufficient to overthrow humanity."

"There you are wrong," said Gustavus sonorously. "They will unite with Lilith and then, when they have made Demogorgon ruler, the Shapeshifter and Lilith will overthrow him before he can reduce the earth to desolation and rule it themselves."

"We cannot stand against all three!" exclaimed the King.

A Dwarf clad, not in the tunic and trews of his fellows, but in a sumptuous robe, leaned towards the King and stated, "You can, now you have the Wand of Merlin."

"If I used the Wand of Merlin as a weapon, I would slay half the creatures on the earth," snapped the King. "No act could justify such a thing. The end, Baldulf, does not justify the means. What! Would you have me act the human politician?"

"I have an idea," said Caroline, a little shyly. "You folks say that in order to rescue Demogorgon from his prison, they need to find a princess with a star on her shoulder to sacrifice. Maybe we could find her first."

"How can you find her?"

"Have you ever heard," wondered Thomas, "of the Internet?"

"We have no such devices in Logres," said the King, "but you and your companions could use it. Yet it will dawn on the Shapeshifter to use it too. However, aught is better than naught. Do what you can on your instruments."

Gustavus rose. Gavin noticed he seemed to be acquainted with the etiquette of the court, if it could be called that. He thanked the King for their meal and said that now they would return home.

"You will need to arrive before your absence is noted," the King observed. "Not far into the woods there is a tunnel through space. I will provide you with an escort of Dwarfs to take you thither. It will bring you for there to Petworth in but a moment. From thence you must fare on your own. For now I bid you goodbye. We shall meet again."

The children, accompanied by a small bevy of Dwarfs, left the wooden palace.

Chapter Eighteen

A tunnel through space is a device that you enter and then emerge at a place some distance away. It is sometimes referred to as a *wormhole*, though it does not contain worms. To this our band of heroes went with an escort of Dwarfs, in case the Goblins of the woods attacked again. However, nary a Goblin was seen.

The tunnel brought them out in a country lane near Petworth.

"Maybe we could find the Csardas and drive back in that," suggested Caroline.

"Maybe we could go to the Professor's house and get Katy to drive us back," suggested Thomas.

"Maybe we could get the Hillford Bus, which I see just coming up the road," suggested Gustavus and all had to admit this was by far the most sensible idea.

All of the children were tired. What I can only describe as the rich experiences of the day had somehow poured a lifetime's excitement into a few hours. Caroline promptly fell asleep when she sat down on the bus. So did Thomas who, while wide awake looked as if he could take on the world and then kick it, seemed to look awfully childish when asleep. Gavin remembered him as a baby. He had looked just like that. Except that when he was a baby, he hadn't been wearing glasses.

I will not describe their bus journey, as I have no wish to bore you with details of hedges, singing blackbirds and the sound of the bus. But Gavin's thoughts are another matter.

You see, Gavin had this feeling that he lacked personality. Gustavus, being a sort of magical individual, stood out from the crowd. Caroline had cheery, sparkling character. Thomas, with his ever-ready responses to everything said, was always the centre of attention. But what had he to recommend him? Very little, or so it seemed. Then a thought struck him. *He was growing into Father.* Father was always overlooked and passed over. He didn't seem to mind. But perhaps he did. Father, in his corner of the room at which conversation was rarely directed and whose contributions to any discussion were largely ignored, might be feeling miserable and neglected. Gavin resolved to include Father in the conversation rather more. The trouble was this tendency of Father's to answer in grunts.

"Do you know," said Gustavus, who decided they had been silent long enough, "that the Prof is able to time travel?"

"Like in a time machine?" wondered Gavin.

"Yes, but he doesn't need a machine," Gustavus answered. "He uses this stuff you sniff."

"Are you sure he's not a druggie?" Gavin asked.

"No, he's not," replied Gustavus, a touch of impatience in his voice. "You see, we live in a universe that is a space-time continuum. It started with the Big Bang and unrolled like a roll of cellotape to the end of time. One can discover how to move along the tape into the future."

"Has he ever gone there?" Gavin asked.

At this juncture Caroline let out an almighty snore, more of a snort in fact and a number of the passengers started laughing. She woke up.

"What are you all guffawing at?" she wondered.

At that, the bus pulled into the station at Hillford.

Chapter Nineteen

At this stage, Gavin reckoned the adventure was at an end. They had found the Wand of Merlin, delivered it safely to King Lamorak and there was nothing further to be done. He would keep in touch with Gustavus, of course, to find out how things were progressing, but he felt he had had enough adventuring for the time being.

Next morning, the skies opened. It is not unusual in England for rain to fall in July, but this was fairly exceptional. Gavin was rather tired, having spent the best part of a night up and doing earlier in the week and all he wanted to do was relax.

It was not to be. About half way through breakfast there was a frenzied thumping on the door. Father shambled out and the drenched form of Mr Gascoigne came within. Instead of discarding his saturated coat, he shook himself in the fashion of a dog. Rover, the real dog, lying in his basket, received much of the water and yelped protestingly. Mr Gascoigne wore a bowler, or as Caroline would say a derby, hat, but made no effort to remove it.

"It's gone," he said. "They've taken it."

Gavin suddenly had an uncomfortable feeling. The Csardas, which they had pinched from outside Mr Gascoigne's door, was still at Professor Vilnius' house in Petworth.

"Joyriders!" bellowed Mr Gascoigne, his gaunt but wrinkled face showing an increasing fury. "The curse of modern society! They'll probably find its burnt out frame somewhere. How am I to get anywhere?"

Gavin's parents had by now figured out what he was talking about.

"Someone's stolen your car," exclaimed Mother, with the triumphant air of a person who had deciphered Etruscan.

"My car!" responded their soaking neighbour. "Of course someone's stolen my car. What else do joyriders steal? Roller skates? Pogo-sticks? Tricycles? Of course someone's stolen my car."

Gavin and Thomas exchanged glances. They were slightly guilty glances, but as their parents never looked properly at them, they did not guess that their children might be involved.

"Have you contacted the Police?" wondered Father.

"Of course I have!" thundered Mr Gascoigne. "They said they would send someone around. Do you know who they said was probably responsible? Joyriders!"

At that moment there was another knock at the door.

"Answer that, Gavin," said Mother. Gavin complied.

At the door was a very wet postman.

"Packet for this number," he said. "You'll hafter sign for it."

The postman was not young as postmen go, wrinkled of face and grey of moustache and eyebrows. Gavin signed and the postman limped back to the gate.

"Look, it's addressed to *The Head of the Family*" observed Thomas, who had accompanied Gavin to the door. "Mother, there's a parcel for you."

Thomas hadn't meant to upset Father. It was just that he always somehow considered Mother the Head of the Family, as she was always bossing Father about. Father, although he understood where Thomas was coming from, could not helped feeling a little piqued.

Mother picked up the parcel and was about to unwrap it when Thomas suddenly seized it from her, rushed to the back door and flung it out into the back garden.

"Thomas, what *are* you doing?" demanded Mother.

A moment later there was an almighty explosion followed by the emission of a green, gaseous, noxious substance into the air.

This was enough to distract even Mr Gascoigne from his preoccupation with joyriders. The back windows were blown in. Likewise, the glass panel in the back door and several bits of wall.

"Get outside," barked Father, it being one of those rare moments when he could assert himself. "There's some kind of gas coming from it."

Out they all shot into the pouring rain, Rover leading the way.

****

It was Katy who eventually discovered Constable Gashforth, still asleep in the ditch outside the Professor's house. It was raining heavily in Petworth as in Hillford, but the rain seemed to have no effect on the sleeping policeman. Katy got out of her car and went to help him. A sudden creepy thought crossed her mind - could he be dead? No, he was breathing. Katy shook him gently by the shoulders.

Constable Gashforth was dreaming. He was dreaming he was trudging across the steppes of Russia, with a Russian choir singing *Stenka Razin,* a gentle Russian folksong about a man who murdered his wife by throwing her into the river, in the background. Suddenly, in his dream he was being shaken wildly by a fierce creature that seemed like a tusked ape. The ape was in Cossack attire. He threw up his hands and grabbed its shoulder, tearing said Cossack attire. Then he awoke.

"You were having a nightmare," explained Katy, as Gashforth came to terms with his surroundings. "Yore soaking wet. Have you been here all night?"

"I-I don't know," said Gashforth. "Oh, Miss, I am sorry, I've torn your blouse."

In thinking he was grasping the his assailant's shoulder, he had grabbed Katy's and ripped her top. He noticed something a little strange on Katy's shoulder beneath. It was a birthmark in the shape of a star. But he had never seen anything like the star's colour before.

Chapter Twenty

It was still pouring with rain on Hazel Street, where Gavin lived. However, the whole street had been evacuated and cordoned off. The Police had responded rapidly when the question of possibly toxic gas had arisen. Men in white protective overalls (or coveralls, as Caroline would have called them) with instruments that went bleep were patrolling slowly up and down. Mother turned thoughtfully to Thomas.

"How did you know there was something like that in the parcel?" she asked.

"Just a hunch," said Thomas evasively.

Gavin pulled him to one side. "Just a hunch," he said unbelievingly. "How did you really work out what it was?"

Thomas lowered his voice. "Didn't you notice the postman?" he asked. "He was limping. Like the Shapeshifter."

"Gee, you're smarter than Sherlock Holmes," said Caroline admiringly.

"I like to think so," Thomas placidly replied.

Mrs Schneider, from across the road, said she didn't know what things were coming to.

Mr Gascoigne approached a police officer. "Do you think the parcel could have been sent by joyriders?" he enquired.

The policeman said he thought it unlikely.

"At least nobody was hurt," observed a man with hardly any hair.

A disgruntled looking old lady limped away.

****

Some time later that day Samson Strange stood facing the strange mirror in his house at Petworth. His face bore an expression of extreme dissatisfaction.

"Mirror," he began, "I would speak with you."

Out of the swirling mist and grey shadows on the mirror, a face appeared. Well, not just a face, more a whole head, but there seemed to be no body. If there was, it was hidden by the cloudy surface of the Mirror.

"What would you, Sorcerer?" asked the Mirror.

"The Taylors seem indestructible," complained the Shapeshifter. "I don't know how they survived my attempt on them this morning."

"I don't know either," replied the Mirror. "I am merely an oracle, my sole function to prognosticate obscurely. Had you consulted me beforehand, perchance I could have told you your attempt would not have succeeded."

"And then there's my leg," continued the Shapeshifter. "I had Alvis dig the pellet out, but it still hurts like bedamned and shows no sign of healing."

"Again, I am but an oracle, no physician," supplied the Mirror.

"Tell me this then and tell me clearly," the Shapeshifter demanded. "Will I defeat the Taylors of Hillford?"

"If you seek them in the right place," answered the Mirror.

The Shapeshifter stomped out of the room, as much as you can stomp and limp at the same time.

****

It was clear that some of the Taylors' house would need the attention of builders, plasterers, glaziers and painters. Father decided they could not continue in their present house while the repairs were being conducted. He looked glumly out of the hole where once the back wall of the sitting room had stood at the men in their SOCO-suits still collecting forensic evidence.

"Apart from anything else," he said, "we wouldn't be safe here. That lunatic might come back."

They had been assured by the Royal Mail that the deliverer of the package had been no employee of theirs. Father decreed that they move to a cottage near the little village of Padhurst, which belonged to Aunt Dinah. Aunt Dinah had told them it would be all right and had said she might drop in from Haslemere to see them. This was not something that the family greatly desired.

So it was that they packed hasty suitcases. I don't mean that the suitcases were hasty, the packing was. Mr Blackman said he would keep an eye on the house while they were away.

It had been revealed that the gas was now gone, probably evaporated. The residents of Hazel Drive were allowed to return to their houses, which they did with much relief. Mr Gascoigne asked if there had been any progress with the hunt for his missing Csardas. He was told another department was looking into that. The Taylors piled into the car and it went off with a purr. A couple of journalists took photographs of it and a local TV outfit was just turning up.

Gavin spoke to Thomas *sotto voce*.

"We'll have to return old Gascoigne's crock," he said.

"No, they'll soon find it," said Thomas. "I'll ring Gustavus when we get in and tell him what's happened."

Gavin felt that, as the older, he should be doing any ringing, but, on the other hand, he was suffering from a kind of post traumatic stress disorder. It isn't every day you have your sitting room window blown in.

Gustavus, meanwhile, had also thought of the Csardas and had taken the bus to Pulborough early that morning. He had turned up just as Katy was helping a still rather stupefied Constable Gashforth into the house. He too saw the curious mark on her shoulder.

"This is too much to be a coincidence," thought Gustavus, helping Katy move the bemused policeman. "That orphanage must specialise in handling of children people want kept out of sight. It is very unlikely that *two* people would have birthmarks on their shoulder in an unidentifiable colour and the shape of a star. The only drawback is that Katy isn't a princess. But how do we *know* she isn't a princess? How did she come to be in the orphanage? The orphanage were probably told, when she reached sixteen, to make sure she settled down locally so the Shapeshifter would know where she was when it came to making his sacrifice. Only he might not make the sacrifice now as he hasn't got the Wand of Merlin. King Lamorak will have to see that he doesn't get it back. Still, it should be safe in Logres."

"What are you pondering over there?" demanded Katy. "Go and put the kettle on while I look after this pore policeman. Do you want to ring your station to tell them where you are?"

Constable Gashforth, who was returning to normal consciousness slowly, allowed that this might be a good idea. At that moment there came a knocking at the door. Gustavus went over to answer it.

There, standing in the porch, was a Dwarf.

"King Lamorak sends word to the Professor. All is lost," he cried. "The Wand of Merlin is gone."

Chapter Twenty-one

The Taylors' car made its way out of Hillford, passed through Petworth and was soon in the countryside. Green hedges zoomed past as they made their way westwards. Aunt Dinah's cottage was at the bottom of a hillside. Mother was grumbling that both parents would have to commute to work. She would get the train from Horsham, she stated. But it was some distance to Horsham. Father said he would take her there in the car and then proceed to his own work. Mother said she had always said they needed a second car. Father mumbled something about expense.

They actually passed by the house where the Shapeshifter lived, but there was no sign of him. Gavin's mobile rang.

"This is Gustavus," came the voice at the other end. "Disaster has struck. Someone's stolen the Wand."

"So much for King Lamorak's security system," said Gavin.

"Sounds like the Shapeshifter's been active again," murmured Gavin. "Does that man never take a day off?"

"Yes, but he couldn't get it back - the Dwarfs would be on the lookout for him."

"Remember, he can shift shapes," Gavin pressed. "Maybe he was looking like a limping spider."

"Gavin, turn that mobile off." rebuked his Mother. "You're distracting your Father."

Father had been quite undistracted, but knew better than to enter an argument where Mother was concerned.

Mother complained that she had one of her headaches, brought on by the stress of the day. Gavin and Thomas tried to exchange their ideas in muted tones, but Mother told them not to whisper, as she always suspected they were plotting something while they were whispering. Father maintained that silence in which he had these many years found safety. Aunt Dinah's cottage came into sight.

It was built some way back from the roadside and there was a field green with tufty grass and a hillock behind it. The building was mercifully free of Aunt Dinah, who had threatened to turn up to settle them in. Aunt Dinah was a fussy old dame whose idea of *settling* was in fact very unsettling. Mother led the way to the door with purposeful strides, father following, gasping under the weight of two suitcases and the children, with smaller suitcases, followed. Rover frisked around them, glad to be unburdened with any suitcase at all.

When they had unpacked, Father suggested he make a cup of tea. Mother felt that would be good for her headache, as she sank into an armchair and drew her hand soothingly across her brow. Father busied himself with the kettle.

Outside the cottage a rather strange personage was approaching. He wore a long coat that looked as if it had seen better days, bound around the waist with a piece of string. He was an old man with grey hair and a number of (but not too many) wrinkles. He carried a staff in his hand and had a pleasant look on his face. He had a white beard, trimmed to a V-shape. For the benefit of the reader, he did not limp.

Coming to the front door, he knocked and Mother answered it. She looked on her visitor with some distaste. This was a *tramp* and, in Mother's eyes, this made him a *wastrel* and *ne'er-do-well*. This was a class of person which Mother viewed with firm disapproval.

When the man spoke, he had cultured tones and a Welsh accent. Mother had always believed it impossible to combine the two.

"Good morning, madam," said the tramp. "I saw you moving in and I wondered if you could spare a cup of tea and perhaps a sandwich for a travelling man."

"You're *begging*," said Mother disdainfully. "Why do you lower yourself to such a level?"

She obviously judged from his cultured tones that he had not always been such.

"I beg, Madam," replied the other, "because I am a beggar. Were I a cobbler I would cobble, a baker I would bake and a hunter I would hunt. But being a beggar, I beg."

Father, in the background, had been rather taken by the man's peculiar speech, so he said, "Oh, for goodness' sake, invite him in, Catherine, and give him a cup of tea."

So it was that the travelling man was sat down at the kitchen table and a cup of tea, together with a sandwich (ham and mustard), was provided. The two boys were a little intrigued by him.

"What's your name?" asked Thomas, who was always the more forthcoming of the two. Gavin usually had a tendency to hang back in the presence of strangers. *That's my trouble,* he told himself. *I'm too shy. I should be more outgoing.*

"I am called Emrys," said the old man. "That is a Welsh name coming ultimately from a Greek word meaning *undying.*"

"Don't you die, then?" Thomas wondered.

"I haven't yet," said Emrys, taking a bite of his sandwich.

There was a thunderous knock on the other door. The cottage, I should explain, had two doors. Both were in the front. No, I don't know why.

"See who that is," said Mother in languid but pained tones.

Gavin wandered over and admitted two police officers in plain clothes who had come to interview them about the explosion at their house. Father was slightly annoyed. He had thought an inspector at least would be assigned to their case, but these were merely two detective constables. The fact that one was called DC Clodd didn't heighten his confidence. The other, DC Sprangle, had no hair on his head, but had compensated for this with a walrus moustache. They asked the sort of questions you would expect, but they were particularly interested in the fact Thomas seemed to have known the parcel was dangerous.

"I intuited it," said Thomas, using a word he had recently learned.

Gavin realised that this wouldn't really satisfy their interrogators.

"I think what Thomas means is that the postman wasn't the usual one, so he thought something was amiss."

At that moment there was another knock on the door. Father opened it to reveal the form of Samson Strange.

"Catherine," he cried, "I heard on the news about your house and the explosion. I came around to see if there was anything I could do to help. Your neighbour, Mr Blackman, gave me your address."

"And who might you be, sir?" enquired DC Clodd.

"Don't you recognise him?" asked Mother. "That's Samson Strange."

"You mean the famous poet who might be the next Poet Lorryate?" asked DC Sprangle, who moved in what he believed to be cultured circles.

"The same," replied Samson Strange stiffly.

"I am a great affishonado of your poetry," informed DC Sprangle. It was somehow clear from his intonation that, while his vocabulary was wide, his spelling needed attention. "I remember reciting that poem *Apocalyptic Babble* at the office party. That was just before you threw up, Clodd," he added, turning to his companion.

"Well, I think we're just about finished here now," said Clodd, who seemed anxious to bring the conversation to a close. "Mrs Taylor, we'll let ourselves out."

They didn't say anything to Father who, as was his wont, had once again been overlooked.

Gavin had been watching the old man, Emrys. He was staring at Samson Strange alias the Shapeshifter with eyes which could not be described as narrowed, but were certainly interested. Before Samson Strange said anything to him, he rose and departed quietly, so that his leaving was not really noticed.

"It's so *kind* of you to come, Samson," Mother enthused. Actually, she would far rather have relished a rest than a visiting poet on so trying a day, but she had to keep in with Samson Strange. "Harold, make Samson a cup of tea, there's a dear."

"No, no, Catherine," said Samson Strange with an expressive wave of the hands. "I don't want to put you to any trouble."

But Father was already filling the kettle. Samson, on Mother's invitation, lowered himself into a chair. He moved the chair so that it faced the boys.

"And I see your two healthy young men have not been too overcome by the explosion," he said, baring his teeth in a wide smile. Those teeth, thought Gavin, were really rather large. Like great fangs. They were yellowish, not white, almost as though they were composed of ivory, not bone. And they seemed to be getting bigger or at least longer as he looked at them. Suddenly, the teeth seemed to be all he could see, like a great wall of elephant tusks. Then they shrank, growing smaller and he noticed that he and Thomas seemed to be in a dark room. Not a pitch dark room, but a room with enough light to see that there was a desk in front of them with the blackened outline of a skeleton sitting at it and the skeleton had big, ivory teeth.

Where is the Wand, the Wand of Merlin? demanded the skeleton.

I dunno, replied Gavin. *It was stolen from Logres. We thought you had it.*

I? No. Some other has pre-empted me, snarled the skeleton and then it seemed they were shot backwards and were within the room in Aunt Dinah's cottage once more, facing Samson Strange.

He was still smiling, but now the teeth, though large, were not abnormal. He turned to Mother and the conversation took a boring, grownup sort of turn. The two boys wandered outside. In the distance they discerned the figure of the old tramp, Emrys, watching the cottage.

"Did that really happen?" asked Thomas. "Did we really go into that dark room?"

Gavin, who had recently taken to reading science fiction novels, had another idea.

"I think the black room was a part of our unconscious, of which we became conscious for a minute, while we were questioned. And as it was all in the unconscious, the other people in the room had no idea the conversation between us and the skeleton - who was, I presume, the Shapeshifter - was going on."

"One thing puzzles me," said Thomas slowly. "Mother was scheduled to interview the Shapeshifter before we had got involved with Gustavus at all. I'm sure the Shapeshifter arranged it, but how could he know in advance that we would become involved."

"Dunno," said Gavin. "Maybe he's got some way of seeing into the future."

Of course, neither boy knew anything about Samson Strange's Mirror.

Gavin took his mobile from his pocket, rang Gustavus and told him what had happened. Gustavus immediately cried, "Well, if they Shapeshifter hasn't got it, who on earth has?"

Back at the Zuppinger house, all was gloomy. Caroline was grounded. At chez Zuppinger, being grounded didn't just mean you couldn't go out. It meant you couldn't watch television, play video games or even breathe too loudly. Darlene Zuppinger believed that iron discipline forged the perfect child. Caroline stravaged upstairs, lay down on her bed, threw Gunther, her toy stuffed rabbit which she had kept from her earliest years, across the room. Feeling remorseful, she picked him up and cuddled him. Just then her mobile phone rang.

"This is Gusatvus," came a somewhat sombre voice/.

"I'm grounded," whispered Caroline. "My cellphone's supposed to be switched off. I hope Mom didn't hear it ring."

Gustavus told her about the strange encounter of Gavin and Thomas.

"We'll have to meet for a conference," he said.

"Well, we'll have to go there tomorrow," replied Caroline. "I can't go out today."

"Caroline, who are you talking to?" her mother called up the stairs.

Caroline switched off her phone and said in a tone of great innocence, "I was talking to myself, Mom."

I doubt that her mother believed her, but perhaps I am wrong.

Chapter Twenty-two

I am sure you've all been wondering what had been happening to George Fanshaw and his glamorous assistant, Myrtle Singleton. They had been out looking for traces of what her paper, the *Petworth Clarion*, was calling The Beast of Petworth. They had found a number of tracks which seemed to be neither those of cat or dog, nor of their wilder brethren, the fox or badger.

Then, on the night after the fire in Hillford, they found a pronounced set of these unusual tracks outside Petworth in fields running parallel with Grove Lane.

"Do you know," said Fanshaw, "I reckon it's a bally hyena. That's the only thing it could be. I mean, it's certainly not anything made by a moggy."

Myrtle felt that to call a cat a *moggy* was somehow politically incorrect, but she didn't voice her opinion.

Suddenly, from the far side of the hedge there came a Growl. There are growls and growls, but this one deserved a capital G. It was the most terrible noise the pair had ever heard. Then, through the hedge, leaving a large rent in the verdure, bounded the Beast of Petworth in all its horror. Myrtle did not even try to take a photograph. The two turned on their heels and ran. The field they were standing in had many bumps and tussocks, over which our heroes stumbled as they rushed towards no destination, but simply to escape the slavering jaws of the advancing animal. This Beast was faster than they. Soon they could hear the panting of its breath approaching them. Myrtle risked a terrified look behind her and saw that the pustules on the Beast's face were actually pulsating as it ran. A moment later it would have sprung on them.

Then suddenly, from behind a hillock in the field, sprang a huge black cat. To anyone who knew his cats, this was a black panther. It landed beside the Beast and sank its jaws into its back. The Beast uttered an indescribable sound, a mixture of pain and fury, and, half-turning, plunged its own fierce teeth into the hindquarters of the panther. The panther's yowl rose to the very heavens, then it fled, the Beast in pursuit. Over a hedge it jumped, over that hedge the Beast followed, and the pair were lost to sight.

Myrtle sat down, nearly fainting. Then she noticed that Fanshaw had already fainted. With trembling hands, she took out her water bottle, swallowed a mouthful and spilt some over the face of the unconscious Fanshaw. He slowly, as one emerging from a drugged sleep, awoke.

"Gad!" he exclaimed. "Did you see that?"

"Y-yes," stammered Myrtle. "There were two animals."

"People have reported seeing many black panthers in parts of England for years. Black panthers that shouldn't be there. Perhaps they were released by their owners. At any rate, it's lucky that that one turned up." Fanshaw spoke with relief.

When the next day dawned, a rather shaken Myrtle made her way to the offices of the *Petworth Clarion*. She had written an account of her adventures of the night before. The editor, a blunt Yorkshireman named Ethan Garbett, shook his head.

"Ee, lass, I know you want to make your career, but writing fiction like this won't do any good at all. We'd be laughed at by every newspaper that prized its reputation if we printed it."

Myrtle was horrified. Garbett went on.

"Where's your photographs of this? There aren't any. Any reporter who saw sights like this and was worth his salt would have taken a dozen of them. Who's your witness? This Featherstonehaugh bloke who's known to the press as a crackpot and half-wit throughout the county. Nay, we won't print."

And they didn't.

****

On the same morning in Pulborough, the voice of Samson Strange rang out.

"Alvis!"

Alvis appeared. Alvis was one of those butlers whom you didn't have to summon twice.

"I've injured my back," said Strange in sour tones. "Get the Special Ointment."

Alvis knew better than to ask how the injury had occurred. When he returned, the pot of ointment in his hand, he had to apply it. It looked to him as though some wild animal had stuck its teeth into his employer's back. He knew from experience that the Special Ointment would cure it in a couple of hours.

"Do you want me to apply it to your injured leg as well?" he asked.

"No, that's too small a wound to waste the ointment on. I've only a limited supply. Now push off and buttle."

Chapter Twenty-three

I don't think I need to dwell on Mr Gascoigne's delight when the police found and returned his Csardas. He cavorted around the road in excitement, telling every wayfarer about the wondrous efficiency of the police force. He took back all the criticism he had levelled at them, in fact he gave the impression he had never uttered it. He was a happy man.

In another part of the town Gustavus Wilkins was none too happy. With his little band split up, it was hard to keep in touch with them all. Yet he knew there was work still to be done. He had a suspicion that the Shapeshifter knew that Katy was a princess eligible for sacrifice. He felt he should look into Katy's sojourn at the Good Hope Orphanage and perhaps find out where she had come from. He also had to find out what had happened to the Wand. If it hadn't fallen into the Shapeshifter's hands, then who had it?

Caroline was still grounded. Her parents were both out. They hadn't locked her in the house, as this would cause problems if the place caught fire and she needed to escape, but she was under strict instructions not to set foot over the threshold. She was in her bedroom, playing on her PC and feeling disgruntled. She was unappreciated, she thought. If only her parents knew she was saving the world from the evil Demogorgon, then they'd treat her with a little more respect.

She heard footsteps coming up the pathway leading to the front door. The postman, she supposed. Then she heard a noise as though someone were fiddling with a lock. She didn't like the sound of that. Caroline was one of those girls of the intrepid sort. On the landing at the top of the stairs, she paused. She could see the front door from there. She picked up a hammer that was lying on a window ledge. The door started to open. Quickly, she ducked out of sight. If she had to deal with an intruder, she felt ambush would be the best strategy.

The door opened. However, the intruder made no effort to proceed quietly. Perhaps he thought the house unoccupied. Caroline looked carefully around the corner on her door. Then she saw it was her father. It was an unknown thing for Mr Zuppinger to return from work during the daytime. Instinctively, Caroline knew something was amiss. He hadn't even closed the door behind him. She saw him, down in the hall, take a large suitcase from a closet and head for the door. Was he going away somewhere? He hadn't said anything. Before he reached it, a rather suave looking individual entered. He wore a black three-piece suit, reminiscent of days gone by, and a tall black hat.

"Mon cher Monsieur Zuppinger, you are making ze vacation perhaps?" enquired this personage in tones that could only be described as silky.

"Get out of my way," demanded Zuppinger. "Who are you, anyway?"

"You may know me as Monsieur l'Estrange," replied the other. "I have come here for your benefit. The police will be here any second now. All the airports and other ways of departing the country are being watched. You will not get away. When the news breaks tonight, your face will be on every TV screen. Public interest will be vast."

"So what are you offering?" asked Mr Zuppinger. "A safe house?"

"I am offering more than that," replied Monsieur l'Etrange. "I can make the whole business go away."

"Oh, yes?" snorted Mr Zuppinger contemptuously. "How you going to do that?"

"You placed a large sum of money belonging to your employer in an offshore account in Liechtenstein. You accomplish the embezzle. The police are on to you. You have been, Monsieur Zuppinger, ze naughty man."

Caroline drew in her breath, but luckily the pair downstairs did not hear her.

"Yet I can wipe the memories of all who know about this," l'Estrange continued. "At present, only a few police know. Before that happens, because of technical abilities far in advance of anything known to mainstream science, I can cleanse the whole thing from the memories of the people concerned."

"As if I'd believe a yarn like that," said Mr Zuppinger.

"I will prove it to you," continued Monsieur l'Etrange. "Look, you have a wife and daughter, no? I will make you forget their names now."

"Of course I haven't forgotten their names," fulminated Mr Zuppinger. "They're --- they're....."

He wrinkled his brow, he contorted his features, but the memory would not come.

"Gee, you can do it," he muttered.

"Quite so," l'Estrange responded. "And I can do it for you, wiping the memories of these policemen, even removing all relevant data from computers."

How Mr Zuppinger was convinced by l'Estrange is something of a mystery. He was, after all, capable of sophisticated financial fiddling. Even though l'Estrange had demonstrated his power, you would expect a man of such acuity to have reservations. Perhaps l'Estrange was using his paranormal powers to blunt his scepticism. In his position, I would have suspected l'Estrange was using hypnosis to make me forget the names. But perhaps I am more intelligent than Mr Zuppinger.

"What's in it for you?" growled Zuppinger, who had long ago learned that free lunches are not usually available.

"In this you help me," said l'Estrange. "Your daughter has involved herself with other children. They work against me. You will act an my agent, discover what they are doing and report to me."

"Done!" said Zuppinger. "You sure you can do this?"

"It is the small bagatelle," answered l'Estrange in his silky tones. "You are off ze 'ook. However, I do warn you that if you fail me, all memories will return and then it is the hoosegow for you, my brave."

Mr Zuppinger and M. l'Estrange walked from the house. Caroline looked in stealthy fashion around the corner of the door.

I bet l'Estrange has a limp, she thought.

He had.

It is, of course, a shocking thing to discover your father has been up to criminal activity. Caroline sat and thought. Should she tell the others? Of course she should, her father would be spying on them. Her father would be spying on her!

She quickly went to her computer and mobile to check if there were any data on them about their adventures. She expected the first thing her father would do would be to go through her files. She deleted some conversations and some numbers, such as Gustavus', from her mobile. Then, on the house's landline, she made a call to Gustavus. She desperately needed to know what she should do next.

Chapter Twenty-four

It cannot be said of Gustavus Wilkins that he was insensitive. Though he had never had the luxury of a set of parents himself, he knew what it must be like to discover one of yours has been doing what he ought not to have been doing. The thing about Caroline's family was that they had never been particularly close. Her father had always been involved in his business interests with the result that he was usually out of the house or, if he was in the house, he was working on some business deal that left him little time to interact with his daughter, while her mother's chief role in life had been bolstering her father's career. Therefore, this appalling revelation that her father was some kind of crook who had stolen money from his firm had not hit Caroline as hard as it might hit some of us. But she was shocked and upset all the same. Gustavus did his best to comfort her. While they were on the telephone, he arranged another meeting. They would go to Padhurst, a few miles beyond Petworth, which was a village near where the Taylors' cottage lay.

Then Caroline rang Gavin. She had known Gavin for several years and exchanged friendly insults with him for most of that time. Gavin's voice she found rather comforting, as it was familiar. He assured her that everyone had criminal ancestors and that his grandfather had once been arrested for chasing nuns with an axe. This was an interesting story, but I haven't time to tell it to you now.

"Now go and give your rabbit a cuddle," advised Gavin. "That'll make you feel better."

Her rabbit? Her stuffed rabbit? How had Gavin known about her rabbit? She must have told him about it when she was little. What had made him guess she still had it? How did he realise that cuddling it would make her feel better? Well, never mind, the idea wasn't bad. She felt a sudden warmth towards Gavin for suggesting it.

Gustavus was making his way to the hospital. Hillford Hospital is not large. It's what is referred to as a cottage hospital, dealing with minor disorders (not sick cottages). When Gustavus arrived he learned that they still hadn't discovered what was wrong with the Professor and were transferring him to a hospital in Brighton.

Gavin groaned. This was quite a hefty distance away and would make communication more difficult. Dr Vilnius did not like it much either and surveyed Gustavus gloomily through his monocle. (I never told you he had a monocle, did I?)

"There's nothing wrong with my heart, apparently," he told Gustavus. "They tell me I'm talking lucidly, so I'm guessing my brain is all right. Black Death. Yellow Jack and Scarlet Fever all seem to have been ruled out. They are making dubious noises about a number of other things with Latin names, not realising that I speak Latin fluently. If they can't find a cure," he continued in hushed tones, "I've half a mind to time travel into the future and see what they can do there."

"Have you ever travelled into the future?" asked Gustavus. He knew the Professor had said it was possible.

"No," the Professor replied slowly. "I know in theory how it's done, but I know of only one person who has actually done it."

"Who," enquired Gustavus with much interest.

"Merlin Ambrosius, the greatest wizard who lived," supplied the Prof. "Mind you, at times he seemed as mad as a hatter. But what is it the poet Dryden says?

> Great wits to madness sure are near allied
> And thin partitions do their bounds divide.

After the battle of Arthuret, he went out of his mind and became a *gwyllt* who dwelt in the forest. He had a pig to keep him company. Intelligent animals, pigs, thought you wouldn't think so."

"I didn't know the wizard Merlin was also called Ambrosius," Gustavus said.

"Oh, yes, they called him that. You see, in Greek *ambrosios* means the one who lives forever. The Welsh translated Ambrosius as *Emrys*."

The Prof moved about, shifting his position in the bed.

"The Romans called him that because the Ancient Britons said he was kind of a spirit of the land. They referred to Britain as his *clas*, the area of his special rule.

"Now, I've been thinking about our problem. If the Wand has been stolen and the Shapeshifter isn't the one who stole it, that means it has been stolen by somebody else."

Gustavus could not fault the logic of this.

"We must ask ourselves who else would be likely to know of its location," the Prof continued. "Some years ago there was a kind of character in London who sold false relics to American tourists. Among the things he succeeded in prevailing on persons to buy were what he said were William Shakespeare's quill pen, Long John Silver's crutch and a stuffed cat which he claimed had been the property of Dick Whittington.

"However, one tourist smelled a rat when he tried to sell him a pickled eyeball with an arrow in it which he asserted was a souvenir of the Battle of Hastings. This tourist denounced him to the police and he ended up in Wormwood Scrubs.

"When in there, he shared a cell with a person called Algernon Mealyface, who had been a servant of the Council of Magicians and who told him about the Wand.

"Emerging from prison, quite unreformed, this fellow determined to get it. He thought it would bring him immense power which, of course, is true. He searched tirelessly for it and perhaps it was he who found it and sold it to the Shapeshifter. I do not know. He may have known about Lamorak's mini-kingdom. Hearing it was there, he might have stolen it again. He was a very gifted thief."

"What's his name?" Gustavus wanted to know.

"His name is Habakkuk Murdstone," the Prof informed him. "Where he is now, I do not know."

Gustavus pedalled home. When he came to Tandem Road, he glanced into the garden next to his. Holmes and Watson were standing there. They were the owner's West Highland terriers. They barked furiously, as is the custom with West Highland terriers. Gustavus opened his door and went into his house. He reckoned that a man with a name like Habakkuk Murdstone should not be all *that* difficult to track down.

Chapter Twenty-five

"That *horrible* tramp man," exclaimed Mother, returning from a walk.

"Do you mean Emrys?" asked Gavin.

"Yes. I thought when he left the cottage he'd *go*. That's what tramps do. They *tramp*. And when you tramp you go somewhere else. But he's sitting by a tent near the cottage. And you'll never believe this - he has a *pig* with him."

"Why would he want a pig?" asked Thomas, looking up from a book which he had been reading. "Is it a pet or does he plan to eat it?"

"Ugh!" said Mother. "I don't know and I don't care.

Mother was working from home or rather working from borrowed cottage. Father had taken himself off to his office. He liked his office. It was quiet there. He could figure out his figures and no one would disturb him. Especially Mother.

"This bloke sounds interesting," said Gavin. "Let's go up and talk to him."

Happily, Mother had not heard this remark or she would have forbidden it outright. The two boys quitted the caravan and saw old Emrys by his camp in the distance.

A few vigorous footsteps brought them over to him. He looked up. "Oh, it's you two," he remarked. "May I introduce my pig."

The pig's name, it transpired, was Moccos. It grunted at the boys, as though greeting them. "I have a wolf too," informed Emrys, "but he keeps a low profile."

"Doesn't he ever have the urge to eat Moccos?" wondered Thomas.

"He's a vegetarian wolf," answered Emrys. "He eats only vegetarians."

He paused to poke his fire with a stick.

"I believe you've been working with Dr Vilnius," he continued.

"How did you know that?" asked Gavin.

"We wizards have ways of communication," the old man informed him. "Yesterday, I sent a sparrow to communicate with him. His reply was to supply details of you. You see, I had rather gone to earth for a while. Lost touch. But I had picked up rumours that my Wand was in jeopardy and I thought I'd better come out of the woodwork. I have made contact with Gustavus Wilkins."

"Your Wand?" said Gavin. "Are you Merlin the wizard?"

"You're quick," said Emrys, or Merlin as we may now call him. "But I am told that the Shapeshifter has allied himself with the demoness Lilith."

"So we've been told," said Gavin.

"Have you ever seen Lilith? Do you know what she is like?" the old wizard asked.

"No," admitted Gavin.

"I would know where she bides and what are her designs," said Merlin. "Will you go and discover that for me?"

"Certainly," said Gavin, with what he hoped was an air of nonchalance. "Mind you, Gustavus is coming down today and I'm going to have to meet him."

"Oh, you'll be back in plenty of time for that," said Merlin. "Unless," he added a trifle ominously, "something goes wrong."

"Can I go too?" asked Thomas.

"I'd rather only send one," said the wizard. "Your Mother might be a trifle annoyed if *two* of you disappeared."

"Drink this," said Merlin, proferring a decidedly grubby looking bottle.

Gavin suddenly felt a trifle unsure about the matter, but raised the bottle to his lips. I wish I could tell you it had a wondrous and magical flavour, but it didn't taste much of anything. Almost at once, Gavin began to feel drowsy. He lurched forward and Merlin had to grab him to stop him falling into the fire. The inside of his head seemed to be swirling. He saw visions and sights of strange things, of greenery and foliage, of dark and fouldering skies, of windswept plains covered with snow and of islands of tropical luxuriance. Then all seemed to come together and he was in a desert. All the ground was covered with sand, but his way was punctuated by the odd boulder.

He thought at first he was riding a horse, but then he realised it was a camel. As they sped across the sands, the camel turned and looked at him from time to time, without slackening speed. This is something disconcerting, that camels do.

At length they came to a sort of natural formation of rocks. The camel knelt down and Gavin dismounted. He made his way to the rocks and climbed them as quietly as possible, for he did not know what lurked on the other side.

Once he reached the top and looked over, he beheld an astonishing sight. What was undoubtedly Lilith stood on a pillar. She was clad in garments of samite, not in the armour she had worn before, and was, it must be said, dazzlingly beautiful. She was standing on a rocky pedestal in the midst of a valley surrounded by rocks. All about her, seated on the rocks like an audience, was the most horrible bunch of hideous crones that Gavin had ever seen. Their faces were wasted and gaunt and scarred, many boasted wispy beards, their noses were often hooked and their chins pointed. They talked among themselves but their words came out in mere mumbles, incomprehensible to Gavin. They wore rags of much rot, where their arms were visible they were thin as famine victims and, as to their lips, some were thin and cruel, some big and slobbering. They held primitive-looking weapons, spears with stone heads and axes also of stone Then Lilith spoke.

"My sisters," she cried, "that world domination which is rightfully ours is near at hand. We are to unite with the Shapeshifter and bring back Demogorgon. Once he is free again, he will make the world ours and no more will we be exiles from a scornful humanity. Then we will destroy Shapeshifter and Demogorgon alike and the world will be ours alone."

A cheer went up from the assembled hags. I say a cheer, but it was more like a great moan as they raised their voices in a sort of strange delight, strange because it did not reach their faces, strange because its pitch, though it was meant to be a cheer, sounded in some ways like a kind of eerie wail. A bird walked past one of them and she picked it up in her bony hand and stuffed it into her mouth, despite its struggles. Gavin closed his eyes in revulsion and, when he opened them, he was sitting at Merlin's fire with Thomas and the old man.

Chapter Twenty-six

You would think that tracing a man with so singular a name as Habakkuk Murdstone would be quite easy, especially when you have the Internet. Gustavus had the Internet, but nowhere could he find a reference to Habakkuk Murdstone. He found the biblical prophet Habakkuk, a racehorse called Habakkuk's Pride, a Habakkuk Honeybunn who gave children's parties and was really called Joe Fish, but he reckoned Habakkuk Murdstone must have died, changed his name or vanished in a puff of smoke.

Irritated, he called Caroline the next morning.

"Are you allowed out yet?" he demanded, not bothering to give any kind of greeting.

"Yes," said Caroline, in a subdued voice. She hadn't yet got over the fact that her father was a criminal who was now spying on her for the Shapeshifter.

"Then we'll have to go see the Taylors," urged Gustavus. "We've got to see where we go from here."

Caroline gave a sad little affirmative and Gustavus wondered what was the matter with her. When he asked, she reminded him of the sad tale of her father.

They all met up at the cottage in Padford. It was facing the main road, so it was easily discovered. When they arrived on their bicycles, Gustavus and Caroline could see Gavin and Thomas sitting by Merlin's fire. Merlin appeared to be eating a sausage he had just cooked over it. Moccos the pig was sitting nearby, looking on disapprovingly, as though he did not countenance the eating of pork.

"So, we are all here at last," said the wizard. "Now, we can bring each other up to date with what we know."

Which the children did. All were suitably sympathetic about Caroline's father, though they could have done without Thomas's comment that he had always thought Mr Zuppinger looked a bit iffy anyway.

"Thomas meant no offence," said Gavin, giving his brother a severe glance.

"Now I will tell you what I know and you don't," said Merlin, looking, it must be said, a trifle smug, as though he liked having information that others didn't.

"The Shapeshifter discovered where Katy was, shortly after she was born. Kidnapping her, he assumed the shape of a Frenchman who looked from his attire as if he had lived in the time of the Franco-Prussian War, and turned up at the Good Hope Orphanage. He had no trouble in prevailing on Rumball, the supervisor, to take the child until he should have acquired the Wand.

"When she was sixteen, Rumball introduced her to the Vicar of Padford, who was looking for a wife. The Vicar was so kind and thoughtful a man that Katy, whose only experience of men had been Rumball and his dissolute staff, was most taken with him. In due course they married, Rumbball knowing that, as they lived nearby, he could keep an eye on her and report back to the Shapeshifter. In payment, the Shapeshifter kept government officials who might have looked into the state of things at Rumball's residential home, at a distance.

"I discovered that Katy was a descendant of King Golar by the use of a magical technique I picked up from an old woman in Tunbridge Wells," Merlin continued. "I passed this on to old Doc Vilnius, who promptly engaged her as a housekeeper. He wanted to make sure nobody sacrificed her."

"Very good of him," muttered Caroline.

"I believe he gave her some training in magic, which I would not altogether have countenanced," continued Merlin. "And now we have to look for Habakkuk Murdstone, as he possibly has the Wand. I surmise he'll try to sell it, but I doubt that he'll know where Samson Strange lives, even though he'll know that he's the obvious customer. I wonder how he got into Logres? The Shapeshifter, despite his many shapes, would never have got past the spells which protect it. I must go to the New Forest. Come on, Moccos."

"You're not going to walk all the way there?" asked gavin.

Though Merlin looked very spry for a man hundreds, perhaps thousands, of years old, this seemed a somewhat extreme perambulation.

"No, no," said Merlin with a laugh. "I have a motor-bike up the road. Moccos will travel in the sidecar."

And with that he departed, a dishevelled looking figure, with a speedy stride.

The children made their way to the cottage. Mother (working from home again) observed the departure of Merlin with some satisfaction. She offered the children a drink (non-alcoholic) and buns (also non-alcoholic) and then returned to her work, having issued orders not to disturb her.

Caroline's phone rang. It was her father, wanting to know where in tarnation she was. He thought she was still grounded. Now she had slipped out of his sight and that Frenchman might turn up again.

"It's all right," she assured him. "I'm visiting the Taylors."

Mr Zuppinger gave a sigh of relief. She couldn't do much to annoy the mysterious Frenchman there.

There was a knock at the door. Not so much a knock as a frantic pounding. Gavin answered it. Outside stood a very frightened looking man.

"Yes?" Gavin enquired doubtfully.

The man caught his breath and then said, "My name is Habakkuk Murdstone."

Chapter Twenty-seven

So this was the much sought Habakkuk Murdstone, ex-prisoner with magical knowledge, and he looked as though he had had seven bells scared out of him. He stumbled or rather threw himself into the cottage, closing the door by kicking backwards with his foot. The children noticed he had two huge parallel rents in the back of his jacket. He staggered towards a chair and sat down.

"Are you all right?" said Gavin, for Murdstone looked very much as though he wasn't.

"He's had a shock," said Caroline. "He needs a cup of tea with a lot of sugar."

He actually looked as though he needed a keg of brandy rather than a cup of tea, but he spluttered out, "Mr Pighills sez to tell you I'm all right."

Who Mr Pighills might be was a mystery to the children, but Habakkuk Murdstone waited to be handed his tea before he elaborated.

"I live in a flat in Uxbridge," Murdstone explained. Older readers may remember that Uxbridge once featured in an advertisement for washing powder. Others won't.

"Well, Mr Pighills came knocking on my door. *Mr Murdstone, he sez, I've had a message from Dr Vilnius wot is a friend of mine in hospital. He sez yore to go down to Padford and meet some children at the roadside cottage just outside of it and tell them that yore not the thief as stole the wand.* And I sez, *Wot wand is this?* And Mr Pighills he sez, *Blest if I know, but this is urgent.* So I gets into my car and sees this cottage and I thinks to myself, I thinks, *This is a cottage by the roadside, I'll try this one.* So I gets out off the car but before I've took two steps I hear a beating noise and looking behind me I sees this huge bird, bigger than a *heegal*, with outstretched wings swooping down at me so I runs like I was in the Olympics and I feels its vicious talons grab at my back at tear my jacket, but it doesn't get a grip and I reaches this door and here I am. And Mr Pighills sez to tell you as I ain't stole the Wand."

What had happened was that Dr Vilnius had, by some magic art, discovered that Mr Murdstone, who had no telephone, lived next door to Mr Pighills. He had rung said Pighills and given him a message for Mr Murdstone.

Habakkuk Murdstone was in a clear state of flusteration. His breath came heavily in gusts and gasps. The children, however, realised that he bore a message of importance. Thomas looked out of the window.

"I don't see any big birds now," he supplied.

Gavin almost asked if the big bird had had a limp, then he realised Habakkuk would have no way to seeing this. At this moment Mother entered.

"Who are you?" she demanded in none too friendly tones.

"This is Mr Murdstone," explained Caroline, who had a soothing diplomatic voice she used on such tricky occasions.

"He's just had a nasty experience."

"He was attacked by a big bird," explained Thomas.

"Are you all right?" Mother enquired.

"I'm much better now, thank you," said Habakkuk Murdstone rising to his feet. "I'll just get back in my car and drive home."

He quitted the cottage, looked carefully around and made his way down to his car. Happily, he was free from attack by the avifauna.

"What an odd man," said Mother, as his car did a U-turn and disappeared in the direction of Petworth.

When Gustavus and Caroline set off for home, Merlin had not yet returned. When Caroline arrived home, she found her father was uneasy.

"Where have you been all day, Caroline?" he asked.

Caroline knew why he was asking: so he could report back to the Shapeshifter. She felt a growing depression that her father was spying on her in this way.

"Just visiting friends," she said and disappeared into the bathroom, which is every girl's favourite place of refuge.

Chapter Twenty-eight

The next day Gavin and Thomas, who were sleeping in bunk beds, were awakened by the sound of a motor-bike drawing to a halt outside. Thomas, who was energetic by nature, sprang from his bed, while Gavin arose more slowly. Gavin looked at his watch. Seven o'clock. At least his parents would not be about yet to ask awkward questions.

Merlin dismounted from his bike after the children emerged from the cottage. His crash helmet and pair of goggles looked oddly incongruous when combined with his rather grubby overcoat and trousers which seemed to be held up by a length of string. He approached the two boys.

"It's very annoying," he informed them. "This fellow Murdstone didn't steal the Wand at all. In fact, nobody stole it. That fool of a dwarfish magician they keep in Logres was fooling around with it, a dangerous thing to do with that instrument, I can assure you."

He sat down and took out a bundle of sandwiches in a plastic wrapper.

"Anyone want a sandwich?" he enquired.

"What kind of sandwich?" said Gavin doubtfully.

"Cabbage," the wizard informed them. "I've always had a taste for cabbage, since they first introduced it in Tudor times."

"Ugh!" said Gavin and Thomas in chorus, from which you may gather they did not like cabbage.

Merlin, ignoring this response, took a bite, then broke off a piece and gave it to Moccos, who had managed to get out of the sidecar.

"The idiot managed to send the Wand into the future," said Merlin. "I know where it'll go. I've set up a portal stream which carries items of mine into the future to Didymus, a magician of my acquaintance. The only trouble is, to use this stream, I can't travel there myself. I'll have to send one of you."

"Cool!" said Thomas. "Will we go hundreds of years ahead and meet extraterrestrials and unknown interplanetary creatures?"

"No," said Merlin rather firmly. "I have no wish to expose either of you to danger like that. Didymus' end of the portal stream is about twenty years in the future. You shouldn't notice a lot of difference. Whom shall I send?"

He looked at the boys appraisingly. Gavin, despite being curious about the future and what it might hold, even if it were but a score of years ahead, had a kind of nervous feeling in his stomach at the thought of time travel, but Thomas looked quite eager for the experience.

"All right, Thomas," said Merlin. "Put on this ring. Yes, I know it's too big for you, but it'll adjust itself to the size of your finger. There, it's done so. Now, to bring yourself back, just rub the ring. If you're in any danger, whether you have the Wand or not, rub that finger. Understand?"

"Yes," Thomas assured him.

"Right, ready," said Merlin.

He took from the pocket of his overcoat a sort of box with which he twiddled and it suddenly seemed to Thomas he was travelling forward very quickly, for he saw images of things flying past him, but at too rapid a speed to discover what they were. Then suddenly, plump! He was in a place of greenery. Looking around, he saw it was a green field. A cow was looking at him contemplatively. *Moo*, said this peaceful beast.

Thomas found he was lying on the grass and drew himself into an upright position. He looked around. There was a house in the distance. He started to walk towards it.

"You going over there?"

He looked around to see a boy with a friendly face. His clothes were somewhat different from anything Thomas was used to, in that he was dressed in a one-piece suit which seemed to be made of some sort of synthetic material Thomas didn't recognise.

"Be careful," the boy cautioned. "The fellow who lives in that is Mad Old Didymus. He's harmless really. When I was young I used to believe he was a wizard. He's got a wife called Mad Old Becky and she lives in a parrot cage and cackles."

He said the last sentence as though a parrot cage were a very normal habitation for an elderly lady of questionable sanity.

"My name's Stobo, by the way," continued the boy. "Are you going to a fancy dress party? It's just your clothes look as though they date from Noah's time."

"No," replied Thomas. "I'm going to see - er - Mad Old Didymus. I'm Thomas, by the way."

"I'll walk over with you," said Stobo. "I was in Didymus' house once. I fed Becky peanuts. My dad knows him slightly and says he's harmless. I have to be back by late afternoon, though. They're showing the last ever episode of *The Simpsons*."

As they strode across the greensward that lay between them and Didymus' house, Stobo spoke of various things that Thomas could barely understand, coming from a culture twenty years ago. It seemed that school was much easier now, as they could transfer information to your brain electronically. They had discovered there was a civilization on the sea-bed, which was none too friendly. There had been some disastrous results from the melting of the ice-caps, but Stobo didn't elaborate. Stobo's parents had been married on the moon, a custom which seemed to be all the rage. Cars no longer ran on petrol, but on willow wood. Willow trees are renewable, so a new crop of them was grown every year and this meant there was no pollution from cars and fuel was much cheaper. Moreover, willow trees could be grown on the poorest of land, so any farmer with financial difficulties could easily grow a crop on them. The willow fuel slowed cars down too, so there were less road accidents.

Thomas listened with interest to all this until they arrived at the wizard's door. "Come on in," said a recorded voice. "It's not locked."

In fact the door opened before them. They went into a large hall. The only thing curious about it was a very large parrot cage hung from the ceiling and in this was Mad Old Becky, the wizard's wife, who cackled a bit.

Then Mad Old Didymus appeared. He looked comparatively normal. He wore a long robe that looked like a dressing gown. This is because it was a dressing gown, as Didymus always wore one unless he went out.

"I see you're admiring my consort," he said in loud and rolling tones, clearly referring to his wife in the cage. "You may give her a nut, if you wish."

There was a dish of nuts on the table, so the boys diverted themselves by throwing nuts at Becky, who caught them most cleverly in her mouth, cracking them with what must have been rather formidable teeth and spitting out the shells.

"Now, you've come for the Wand of Merlin," said Didymus. He handed it over to Thomas. "I'm glad to get rid of this, I must say. Handle it carefully."

He passed it to Thomas and showed the boys out of the house.

Thomas was just about to bid farewell to Stobo when they saw a couple coming across the swathe of grass towards them.

"It's my mum and dad," said Stobo. "Come and meet them."

As they approached the couple, Thomas felt there was something strangely familiar about them. As they drew nearer, he realised with a shock that the man was his brother Gavin. He had a more grown up face, true, and a small beard, but it was Gavin unmistakably. Then looking at Stobo's mother, he gasped even more. Although she now wore a touch of makeup and her hair was a bit different, he saw at once it was Caroline. They were married. They had been married, according to Stobo, on the moon.

"Look," cried Gavin, "it's Thomas. This must be the time old Merlin sent him into the future."

"Hi, Tom," said Caroline. "What do you think of our little boy. He's your nephew."

But this was all too much for Thomas. He rubbed the ring and disappeared and in a moment he was back in his own time.

Stobo gasped and demanded an explanation. Although his parents had told him stories about being involved with magic when they were young, he'd never believed them. He had thought they were just fairytales.

"But, when he gets back in the past, if he tells you you're going to get married you'll feel you're forced to," said Stobo. "It won't be, like, your own choice."

"He won't tell us," said Caroline.

"How do you know he won't?" Stobo demanded.

"We'd remember if he had," said Gavin.

Chapter Twenty-nine

When Thomas returned from the future, he seemed in a state of some confusion. He handed over the Wand to Merlin and said he wanted to lie down. The complications of time travel are hard to absorb if you're only eight, even if you are as intelligent as Thomas.

"Now," said Merlin, "I have the Wand. For the time being it is safe. But I have no doubt those scoundrels will try to get it back. They'll also try to capture Katy. I think you'd better warn her."

Gavin sent Katy a warning text and went back inside the cottage. Thomas was in his bunk bed, snoring.

****

Caroline noticed that things were coming on well with the rebuilding of the back of the Taylors' house. Workmen were busying themselves about the place, hefting bricks and glass and hardly stopping for a cup of tea. A plumber had been and gone. A representative of the telephone company had checked the telephone. Serious looking electricians had appeared and disappeared.

"Have you nothing to do today?" Darlene Zuppinger asked her husband. "And why are you looking out of the bedroom window with a telescope?"

Henderson Zuppinger looked with irritation at his wife.

"I'm keeping an eye on Caroline," he explained. "She's hanging around the house next door. Places with builders are dangerous."

"Then tell her to come home," his wife said. "Folks round about will think you're a peeping tom."

Henderson Zuppinger had been a little surprised at first by l'Estrange's memory-eradicating powers. But it was not his practice to ponder over how things could be. If something happened, he accepted it, without looking for causes. Although a man of some business acumen, in other respects he was as thick as two short planks. Therefore, he didn't worry about *how* M. l'Estrange could erase memories of Man and Computer. His practical concern was to make sure he didn't restore them once again. The trouble was, he couldn't find out what Caroline was about with her friends when her friends were somewhere else and he couldn't listen in to what she was saying to them. When she had been asleep, he had pinched her mobile phone but had been unable to find any enlightening messages on it.

Then he had a thought. The firm for whom he worked were no strangers to industrial espionage and one of the devices they were no strangers to was the Bugging Device. He could insert one in Caroline's mobile phone. This would enable him to listen into her phone conversations, but the main thing was, even when it wasn't switched on, it would pick up noises, including conversations, around it.

"I'm just off to the office," he told his wife. "I need to pick something up."

"But it's Sunday," his wife protested.

Mr Zuppinger made no response, but entered his car and drove off.

****

It was a very warm Sunday. The sun had cloven the heavens and was warming Merlin's back as he drove along towards Hampshire, the Wand in his pouch and Moccos sitting contentedly in his sidecar. There were quite a few vehicles on the road and one or two drivers noticed that the passenger in his sidecar was not, well, your average passenger. An elderly lady remarked that she was sure having a pig in a vehicle was illegal and did not hear her husband say under his breath, "Well then, my dear, you had better get out." She wasn't the kind of lady who found that sort of remark amusing.

They reached a stretch of the road on the left side of which was a fence and, beyond the fence, a hillside that tumbled downwards towards a small stream. It tumbled quite a long way downwards. In ancient times the stream had been a mighty river that had carved out the valley through which it flowed, but those days were long gone and it had shrunk to its present dimensions many centuries before.

Merlin found himself slightly irritated by the fact that a tractor was now in front of him, slowing him down remarkably, and he couldn't by-pass it because of traffic coming the other way. However, he told himself he was in no hurry. Anyone who had lived as long as he ought to be a stranger to impatience. He saw in his mirror that there was a four-by-four behind him, a little closer than he actually liked, making him slightly uneasy.

Suddenly the four-by-four made as if to pass him by, oblivious of any oncoming cars that might be a danger. In fact, it moved at a highly perilous speed. Before Merlin realised what had happened, it crashed into the side of his motor-cycle, sending him flying through the fence, so that he and it rolled down the hillside to the small stream below.

The four-by-four's driver, a large man with a small forehead and jutting jaw at once pulled to a halt, as did several cars behind him. As Merlin and his bike hit the stream, the driver (and several other drivers) went running down the hill. The driver of the four-by-four, having exceedingly long legs, far outsped the others and reached the form of the unconscious Merlin, half in the stream and half out. He was followed by a Mr Entignapp, who saw him pull Merlin from the waters, but, instead of trying to revive him, he started searching through his pockets.

"My God," thought Mr Entignapp, "he's trying to rob him."

The driver, however, took nothing out of the wizard's pockets and, as Mr Entignapp came up to him, he could hear him muttering, "Where is it? Where is it?"

The driver undid Merlin's coat and tried to look through his trouser pockets, but Mr Entignapp wasn't having that.

"Hey!" he called to the other drivers who had followed him. "This chap's trying to rob him."

The four-by-four driver apparently found nothing in Merlin's pockets, then leapt to his feet as Mr Entignapp reached him. He pushed Mr Entignapp over and raced back up the hill. Another driver said, "I've called an ambulance." The four-by-four, with its driver back, now drove off at some speed. Nobody thought to take the number on its license plates. A crowd of would-be rescuers surrounded Merlin.

Merlin groaned and ejected a stream of water from his mouth.

****

We will now leave Merlin's mouth and look for another. In a bunch of bushes, the Wand held firmly between his jaws, where no one could see him, stood Moccos the pig. A mental stab came to him from Merlin, urging him to take the Wand to the cottage where Gavin and Thomas were. The pig understood. For centuries he had been the companion of Merlin, from the time when Merlin had gone mad after the Battle of Arthuret. That time, his sister Ganieda had healed him, restoring him to the observatory whose construction he had overseen centuries before, which the Ancient Britons called the Giants' Dance and moderns termed Stonehenge. But from time to time the madness had returned, like an unwelcome guest. Moccos and Merlin had a means of communication, mind to mind, and this now told him where to take the Wand.

Meanwhile, many people had come down from the roadside to help the wizard to come to the hospital for a checkup, though he resisted and shouted that he was hale. They paid him no heed, but their hands grabbed him and pulled him, trying to get him back up the hill to the road. Then the many hands became too much for Merlin, the claustrophobia caused by all these people around him, grabbing at him, pawing at him, pushing him, hands everywhere, bringing his madness on again. With a great cry he tore himself loose from his would-be helpers and, raising his hands like some prophet, bellowed out:

Lost and lorn was I in the woods of Caledon,
My garments rent by the taloned sleet,
Companions had I none, save a wolf and a pigling,
My bed the moss and undergrowth of the woodland,
The soughing of the wind constantly through the trees,
The cries of harrier and buzzard above my head.
While Rhydderch's men pursue me, who shall call him
generous?
By his fireside in Alclud he sits while I hear
The music of his hounds pursuing me
As the hawk would the hare across the field.
Get ye gone, ye sons of screeching,
Leave Merlin to the wilderness and wood.

Nobody understood a word of this, as it was uttered in the Ancient British speech, the ancestor of Welsh. As he spoke, he waved his arms about frantically as though he were some kind of frenzied ape. The onlookers stood well back. They heard the siren of the ambulance approaching. Merlin turned about and tore off into the distance, roaring and bellowing as he raced and none tried to stay his progress. He sped through the nearest hedge and was lost to sight.

Chapter Thirty

That night Thomas explored the cottage attic, largely out of boredom. Gavin was watching something uninteresting on television, Mother was working at her word processor and Father was being obscure in a corner. When he got up there with the aid of a ladder, Thomas was interested to note that it must once have been used as an actual room. The floor had been filled in, making it safe to walk in. However, it had clearly been used merely as a store room for some time. There was a box which seemed to contain old shoes in the corner and next to it a box of fireworks. Thomas decided to leave these alone. You didn't meddle with fireworks - dangerous things. Arabella Gumpert, a girl at his school, had got hold of some once and blown off her nose and a finger. The nose had not been anything much to look at, but you'd be surprised how much you miss your nose when it's gone. Cobwebs were everywhere, in particular profusion over the skylight window. Perhaps the spiders had liked to sunbathe. Thomas forced it open after something of a struggle, displacing many a web as he did so. He looked out. The evening was becoming chilly, so he looked in again. Then he looked out again. Had he seen aright? Merlin's pig with something in its mouth was approaching.

"We can't let Mother see that," thought Thomas. "She hates pigs."

He proceeded downstairs and gave Gavin a signal that he must attend by pulling his ear. The two of them went out to find

Moccos gazing up at them, the Wand of Merlin in his mouth. Gavin took hold of it quickly.

"Something must have happened to Merlin," Gavin said. "We'd better telephone the others."

Which they did.

"Where are we going to put Moccos for the night?" wondered Thomas. "Mother would never let him into the house."

"There's a kind of garden shed at the back. He could sleep there," suggested Thomas.

The shed was no garden shed, because there was no garden, but only a field, behind the cottage. But it was a shed nonetheless.

"We'll have to get him something to eat," suggested Gavin.

Moccos understood the word *eat*. Pigs are intelligent animals, as I said before, and over the centuries Merlin's faithful pig had picked up a number of human words. When he heard the word *eat*, Moccos oinked joyfully.

"What do pigs eat?" wondered Thomas.

"Food," replied Gavin.

Further joyful oinks followed at the word *food*.

With Moccos safely ensconced in the shed, the boys went into the kitchen and helped themselves to whatever they could find and would hopefully not be missed. Mother was too absorbed to notice what they were up to. Father showed no interest, even when he noticed Gavin passing him carrying several carrots.

The provender having been supplied to Moccos, the boys went back inside. Gavin's phone rang.

"I'll come down to your place tomorrow," said Gustavus. "If anything has happened to Merlin, this could be serious."

Meanwhile, in Hillford that night, Henderson Zuppinger, villainous businessman, removed his daughter's mobile phone from her pocket and inserted his listening device. Now, all he had to do was bring her to her friends.

****

"Paris, Darlene."

Mrs Zuppinger gazed quizzically at her husband across the breakfast table. He was usually to be seen fiddling with a calculator at breakfast, not discussing European capitals.

"I have to go to Paris, on a business trip," Mr Zuppinger announced. "I'll only be gone for a couple of days."

"But you know I have to go to a team-building exercise in Crawley for the next two days," protested Darlene. "Who's going to look after Caroline? We can't leave her with Thelma."

Aunt Thelma had returned from hospital and had been a very demanding recuperant.

"I was thinking maybe we could leave her with the Taylors in their country cottage," Mr Zuppinger said smoothly.

Darlene considered. The Taylors were, after all, responsible people.

"Okay, give them a ring and see if they'll take her," she replied.

At once Mr Zuppinger telephoned the Taylors. He was lucky to get Father, rather than Mother. Mother might have hemmed and hawed, considering children a nuisance and more children than necessary an unnecessary nuisance. Father, on the other hand, was unbothered by children, as he never let them bother him.

"Of course, Henderson, bring her down," he invited at once.

So it was that Caroline was roused from her bed, much to her displeasure. She was told she had five minutes to dress, five minutes to eat her breakfast and three minutes to use the bathroom. Half an hour later she was speeding in her father's Coppola towards Padhurst.

"Gee, Aunt Thelma sure wasn't pleased to be left on her own," Caroline reflected. "Still, I'm glad I'm not there with her. Oh, darn, I've left my cellphone at home!"

Henderson Zuppinger paled beneath his pallor. There would be no use bringing Caroline to Padhurst without her bugged mobile phone.

"Don't worry," he croaked. "We'll go back and get it."

"There's really no need, Pop," she informed him. "I was never a great one for phoning and texting."

"No, no," said her father. ""You must have it - in case we need to call you."

So the duplicitous Mr Zuppinger turned his Coppola around and returned to his domicile.

Darlene had already left, so Henderson told Aunt Thelma the purpose of his mission. Aunt Thelma wasn't much impressed.

"Coming all the way back here for a stoopid cellphone," she snorted in contempt. "We didn't need such things when I wus young. Back in those days----"

"Back in those days you had to use big umbrellas to keep the pterodactyls off," said Caroline, grabbing the mobile. She herself hadn't thought it worthwhile to make the journey back. She wasn't one of those people who cannot live without a mobile phone, cannot believe any society ever functioned without mobile phones, cannot believe in a world where once phones were never mobile. Her father, who was jittering around nervously, on the other hand, deemed it essential that she have it, for reasons we all know.

As the Zuppinger car drew up in front of the cottage outside Padhurst, Father was just departing for Horsham, Mother with him. Mother had elected to drive, for Father's caution on the road was a source of irritation for her. Mr Zuppinger decanted Caroline and her solitary bag from the car and she entered the cottage. Gavin had just received a text from Gustavus, saying he would come down after visiting the Prof, who hadn't yet been moved to Brighton General Hospital. For some reason, whenever the Hillford staff were about to put him in an ambulance and send him off, something always cropped up to prevent them. However, the Prof was not cured of his little ailment, whatever it was, yet. Whenever he sought to quit his bed and walk, he felt dizzy. One of the doctors, Julian Fair,

MB, BCh, BAO, had actually almost figured out what was the matter. But we'll come back to him later.

Caroline demanded food, preferably biscuits or, to use her own terminology, cookies.

"There isn't a packet of them in the place," said Thomas. "Gavin, nip into Padhurst and get some. My legs are so little it would take me far too long."

"All right," said Gavin. "I'll go by the river, not by the road. Noisy place, trucks everywhere."

Gavin liked peace and quiet in the morning.

"I had hardly any breakfast this morning," Caroline complained. "I wonder why Pop was so eager to get rid of me."

The said Pop at that moment was renting a room in a B&B in Padhurst. In fact, the only B&B in Padhurst. Mrs Lindwash, proprietress, was pleased to get a guest for a couple of days, as she had a room that was going to be vacant until then. Mrs Lindwash didn't altogether like the look of Henderson Zuppinger, who she guessed was a businessman of low moral fibre. Mrs Lindwash wasn't far off the mark.

He set up his equipment to hear Caroline and Thomas speaking. Gavin must have gone out. Caroline was giving Thomas a rather boring description of her home in Boulder, Colorado. Thomas was trying to change the subject to something more interesting. In due course Caroline went on to tell him about Aunt Thelma's Dark Secret, which I cannot tell you because it's a Dark Secret. Mr Zuppinger, growing bored, wondered where Gavin was.

Gavin was sauntering along the riverbank. The River Duffar was a rather modest waterway, the sun was out, the weather was pleasant and small fowls were making melody. Then the sky clouded over and he came to the where the bridge should have been, only it wasn't. He noticed that the river seemed to have grown wider and its waters greyer, reflecting the skies overhead.

"What's happened to the bridge?" he wondered.

It had only been a small metallic footbridge. Could you take small metallic footbridges down to repair them? he wondered. An old woman, dressed in a macintosh as though she had anticipated bad weather setting out, was standing where the bridge used to be.

"The bridge is gorn," she said. "They must of took it in for repairs."

"Do you need to get to the other side?" asked Gavin as a big wave splashed up on the bank. *My goodness*, thought Gavin, *I've never seen the Duffar this wild before.*

"Afore we had a bridge here, we used the stepping stones," said the old woman. "See, they're just under the water. But the Council said they was too dangerous and put up the bridge. But I can't get across. These old legs aren't steady enough, with the weather so wild."

Gavin didn't like the look of the river at all, but it was only the Duffar, he'd never heard of anyone drowning in it.

"I'll help you across," he said gallantly.

"That's very kind of you," said the old woman.

She grabbed Gavin's jumper with a grip of steel. Her legs might have been shaky, but her fingers seemed strong as iron. She extended a timorous foot onto the first stone. Once her second timorous foot was on it, Gavin extended his. The stone, being slightly below surface, was slippery under his shoe. Then he brought his second foot on to the stone and the old woman, not waiting for this, moved on to the second stone.

They were at about the middle of the river and Gavin could not believe how long it was taking them, it seemed so wide and they were getting drenched with spray, when a really high wave, which looked as if it should have been in the sea, crashed into them and nearly drove them into the water. Indeed, that is where Gavin would have gone, had not the woman given him a helpful yank. But now the river seemed to be actually attacking them. Large spurts of water lashed against their faces and more dangerously, their legs, unsteadying them as if purposely trying to bowl them over. Another wave struck, sousing both of them and, when it ebbed, it nearly drew the old woman to watery destruction. She reached the next step and Gavin followed, but his shoe slipped so badly on the rock that he fell face forward and bloodied his nose. The old woman managed to help him up.

"We're nearly there," she cried.

True enough, her next step took her to the further bank and Gavin essayed to jump from the last stone. A final burst of water struck him, knocking him into the river, but he managed to grasp the bank and pull himself out of the torrent.

When Gavin was safely out, the weather suddenly cleared up. The tempestuous river became tempestuous no longer. The sun appeared from behind the rain cloud that had masked it. Standing next to Gavin was not the old woman, but a tall woman of about six feet with golden her and rich clothes of white samite decorated with gold. You can't blame Gavin for looking puzzled.

"I am Ganieda, twin sister of Merlin," she replied.

"You've aged better than he has," said Gavin cautiously.

"We were born with him an oldster and me a youngster," Ganieda replied. "As you will have guessed, I am the old woman you helped across the stream. That was a test to see if you were generous and valiant enough to defeat the Shapeshifter and well have you proven yourself. For that, the river was widened and the waters enstormed. You are, in fact, naught less than an heroic leader. Before long, you will be in battle at Logres."

She held up a large leather bag.

"This is a mighty weapon which you must not use until then, even if you be assailed by evil forces."

"What is it?" asked Gavin.

She told him.

Chapter Thirty-one

When Gavin returned to the cottage, the others looked at him aghast.

"You're *soaked*," said Thomas. "Where are the biscuits?"

Thomas produced these while Caroline told him in no uncertain terms to change out of his wet clothes before he died of pneumonia or other damp-related disorder. All expressed curiosity about the large bag, so Gavin had to tell them about Merlin's sister. Ten days before, the others would not have believed a word of it. Now, after seeing so many wonders, they were prepared to believe anything.

In his B&B room, Henderson Zuppinger was trying to figure out what they were talking about. He could only judge that these references to Merlin the magician and a wild and tempestuous river were to a video war-game or a TV series they were watching, so he decided not to report them to Monsieur l'Estrange. When Gavin had changed they started talking, saying they now had *it* here. This sounded more interesting. They meant the Wand, but Mr Zuppinger could only deduce that it was an important object. He rang the number Monsieur l'Estrange had given him.

He explained where the children were and then said that they seemed to have an important object with them.

"You have done well, *mon ami*," said Samson Strange in his best French accent. "*Et les parents* - the parents of the children - are they within ze 'ouse.?"

"No, they've both gone back to work," rejoined Mr Zuppinger.

"*Alors, c'est bon*," said Samson Strange. "Stay where you are. I may need you again."

Samson Strange summoned Alvis.

"I'm off to Padforth," he announced. "In the woods nearby lives a small tribe of Goblins, loyal to my cause. It's about time they were called into action. Bows shall twang, Alvis, and the dogs of war shall be unleashed."

****

Thomas decided he would take Moccos for a walk. He didn't think you normally took pigs for walks and he was not far wrong, for a farmer's aim is to make his pigs fat as possible. Moccos, however, was another kettle of fish - or pigs, should I say. He crossed the road and entered some woodland beyond.

"Have you ever hunted for truffles, Moccos," he asked. He had seen a television programme about pigs who searched for truffles. Suddenly Moccos seemed alarmed. An arrow struck a tree near to Thomas. A small man with a red cap and grotesque features rushed out of a bush waving a sword. (It was the small man, not the bush, waving the sword). Moccos dived at the Goblin (for such it was) and bit a chunk out of his leg before he could harm Thomas. The Goblin howled and fell over.

"Back to the cottage, Moccos," cried Thomas, as another arrow flew through the air. "There are Goblins about."

In the cottage itself, Caroline was frowning.

"Gavin, have you noticed that Thomas seems to be giving us odd looks and giggling?" said she. "Do you know why?"

Gavin, who had inherited the ability not to notice things from his Father, didn't.

Just then Thomas, accompanied by a grunting Moccos, tumbled into the cottage.

"Goblins!" he cried. "They look as though they might attack at any moment."

"They must know we have the Wand," said Caroline. "Hide it, so if they capture this place, they'll never find it."

"We'll have to put up a defence," said Gavin, taking charge in an unaccustomed way. He thought for a minute. "Ring the Police," he suggested.

However, they found the landline had been cut and something was interfering with the reception of their mobile phones. Yes, Samson Strange had driven down to Padhurst and fouled up the atmosphere so no phone user in the cottage could get a signal. A crafty Goblin, at his behest, had cut the landline.

Samson Strange felt he had no more use for Mr Zuppinger. He wasn't sure where in Padhurst Mr Zuppinger was and didn't much care. But the memories of the police officers investigating Mr Zuppinger's case were suddenly restored. Once more they knew that Caroline's father was a wanted criminal. He had served his purpose. There is only one word to describe Samson Strange alias the Shapeshifter - he was a dastard. This is an old- fashioned word, but it sums the Shapeshifter up perfectly adequately.

Samson Strange looked at Armugg the Goblin chief.

"Are your forces ready?" he demanded.

"Aye," replied Armugg, who was a Goblin of few words.

Then Samson Strange turned into the Beast. Even the Goblins watched in fascinated horror as his face contorted and reshaped itself into that of some unknown but terrifying monstrosity which was neither cat nor dog, but was covered with oozing pustules, his body burst through his clothes showing itself to be covered in scabious skin and mangy fur, much of it transparent and revealing diseased smoking insides, and his hands and feet became huge, clawed paws.

"Right," said Armugg. "We advance."

Chapter Thirty-two

It was in defending the cottage that Gavin showed his resources as a general. His doubts about his self-worth melted like the snow in springtime when he barked out a series of commands, which neither Caroline nor Thomas thought to disobey.

"Get that box of fireworks in the attic," he told Thomas. "Bring it down here. Caroline, boil a kettle."

Moccos looked as though he wanted to be helpful and clearly had some idea that something was going on. Even Rover the dog, who had been snoozing for most of the morning, stood up, as though he knew foes were at hand. By the time Almugg's little army charged across the road and onto the grassy sward before the cottage, they were ready.

A couple of the Goblins stopped running to shoot arrows, but these did no good whatsoever. They merely stuck in the cottage wall. Then, as in a bunch they came nearer, Gavin stood by three rockets from the fireworks at one window and Caroline at another. They lit the touch paper and the rockets whizzed amongst the Goblins, every time they hit one exploding. Even if they had not wrought injury, the explosions of the fireworks would have been too much for the Goblins, unused as they were to such things. But when the fireworks brought injury and possible death, it was *utterly* too much for them. The Goblins turned and fled, leaving bits blown off them on the ground and one or two whole Goblins who would rise no more. Armugg, who had adopted the crafty strategy of leading from the back of the group, was knocked over by his stampeding followers and nearly flattened by their fleeing feet.

"Fools!" growled the Shapeshifter to himself as, in his dread animal form, he charged towards the cottage door. When he reached this he let out an almighty roar by which even those who heard it from a distance were terrified. He pounded on it with his paws and rent its wood with his frightful claws. It was then that Thomas leaned out of the window above and emptied a bowl of boiling water all over him, water boiled by Caroline on Gavin's instruction.

If the Shapeshifter had roared before, now he screamed as the intolerably hot water seared strips from his skin and fur and actually blinded him in one eye. He screeched again and turned and headed for the wood, seeking water somewhere to soothe the agony which wracked him.

Armugg saw him coming and sought to be helpful, even though his own nose had been broken by the tramplings of his underlings.

"Water that way," he shouted, pointing towards a small pool, but the Shapeshifter was not alone in agony, he was enraged and, passing the Goblin leader he slashed at him with his unretracted claws, leaving a great wound in his chest. Then he dived into the pool.

****

"Well, that's all the rockets used up," said Thomas.

There had only been six of them.

"I've a feeling they won't be back," said Caroline.

A few minutes later a bicycle drew up outside. It was Gustavus Wilkins. He looked with astonishment, even horror, at the remains of the Goblin contingent on the ground. There were two dead Goblins and an array of bits of Goblin scattered all over the grass. Dropping his bicycle by the roadside, he rushed to the cottage and pounded on the door. They had seen him coming through the windows and opened it to let him in.

"What happened here?" he wondered.

Breathlessly, the others told him what had occurred.

"This is far too dangerous," muttered Gustavus. "I should never have involved you. We've got to get that Wand back to Logres quickly."

Caroline looked out.

"There's a couple of Goblins picking up the bodies and the bits," she informed them.

"Yes, they have to," said Gustavus. "They wouldn't want humans to discover them and learn that there really are such things as Goblins outside fairytales."

Each of the children felt somewhat exhausted after the battle.

"I'll take the Wand," said Gustavus. "I'll take the bus from Padhurst to Southampton and get from there by bike to the New Forest. I'm the only one with a bike after all. The person I'm worried about is Katy. What if, after all this, they decide to kidnap her?"

"We'll get to Pulborough somehow," Gavin told him. "Will they let you take your bike on the bus?"

"They better," said Gustavus grimily.

"Can't you magically fly through the air?" asked Thomas, who was always anxious to test the extent of Gustavus' preternatural powers.

"I'm not Mary Poppins," growled Gustavus, "or Peter Pan."

****

Henderson Zuppinger was feeling relaxed. His troubles were at an end. He clambered into his Coppola. He was headed for home. He drove past the cottage being used by the Taylors fairly quickly. Didn't want to be seen from there. He turned into the drive at Hillford, happy to be safe once more. When he went in, he poured himself a glass of whisky. You can see from the spelling it was Scotch whisky, as Irish is spelled *whiskey*. As he took the first sip there was a knock on the door.

He opened this to find revealed two detectives and three uniformed policemen who courteously informed him that they had come to arrest him for suspected embezzlement. Henderson Zuppinger worked out that l'Estrange had betrayed him.

"That *scumbag*," he snarled between gritted teeth.

The scumbag in question, Samson Strange, turned up at his house in a taxi. He was helped in by the driver. Alvis was horrified to see him. He appeared to be scalded all over. He instructed Alvis to draw a bath and fill it will all sorts of magical potions. He would be able to heal his injuries, but just now the pain went beyond description.

Chapter Thiry-three

For the rest of this day - the ninth since these adventures started, if you're counting - nothing much happened. Father and Mother returned from work. An evening meal, healthy if not sumptuous, was consumed. Television was watched. When Father took Rover the dog out for his evening walk, he heard the sound of a pig.

"Someone around here must keep pigs," he thought.

In his shed, Moccos curled up for the night.

Rover, sniffing around the grass, found something edible and swallowed it.

"I don't know what it was," said Father to Mother later, "but it looked like a tiny ear."

"Harold, you have a twisted imagination," said Mother.

Next day, it dawned bright and clear - not that any of our heroes saw it, for they did not awake with the dawn. Luckily, Aunt Dinah's cottage had several spare beds, so they had been able to accommodate Caroline without difficulty. As the morning wore on, all arose for breakfast. I could wax lyrical about breakfast, but it wasn't really worth waxing lyrical about. It was nothing out of the ordinary. Father realised, to his chagrin, that his *Daily Reporter* must have been delivered to the house in

Hillford. Father did not fulminate when he was disappointed. Simply, a look of sublime melancholy overspread his face. He took a drink of tea.

In the house of the Shapeshifter, that worthy had had to spend the night in the bath to heal himself of his multiple scaldings. His anger with the Taylors knew no bounds, but it now occurred to him that he should treat them with more caution. If they could injure him this badly, they were certainly formidable foes. He rose from his medicinal bath and had a think. He must get in touch with the Goblins in the Pulborough region. There weren't a lot of them around there and, if the good burghers of Pulborough knew there were Goblins dwelling nearby, not alone would they have to start believing in magical beings, but they would very likely drive the Goblins from their locality.

"Alvis," he said, "I need a good breakfast to recover from my ordeals of yestersay. Then I require you to drive to Pulborough and leave a message I will give you in the hollow oak outside the town."

After Father and Mother had left, the three children decided the time had come for going to Pulborough, with a view to protecting Katy. When Thomas had departed for the bathroom, Caroline remarked once more to Gavin in a slightly irritated voice, "Why does you're your brother seem to start giggling when he looks at us?"

Gavin was surprised. He hadn't noticed. "I long ago stopped trying to work out what Thomas was thinking," he replied. "Some depths are better left unplumbed and what Thomas thinks is one of them."

Meanwhile, the Shapeshifter had been active, or at least as active as his exhausted frame permitted. The Shapeshifter was beginning to feel a little like the Coyote in the Road Runner cartoons. His schemes to obtain the Wand seemed perpetually to come to naught. Now, remember, while Gustavus was on his way to Logres with the Wand, the Shapeshifter did not know this. He thought it was still in the cottage. He picked up the telephone and telephoned Alfred the Yeggman.

If you don't know what a yeggman is, it is merely another word for a burglar. If you meet someone who, on being asked what his job is, says, "Oh, I'm a yeggman," you will know at once the nature of his nefarious occupation. Of course, Alfred the Yeggman wasn't this fellow's real name. No one knew what his real name was. He spoke in a kind of pseudo-Cockney, but any true Cockney would know it was a put-on accent. Various rumours circulated about his true origins. Some said he was the son of a Royal Personage, some conspiracy theories said he had been constructed in a secret government laboratory and some said his father was a haberdasher in Poulton-le-Fylde. Wherever he came from, there was no doubt he was the most proficient burglar in the south-east. I could give you a list of some of the burglaries he had accomplished, but the Critics would say this would be a Digression, not Germaine to the Main Plot. So I shall leave him on the other end of the telephone, answering the Shapeshifter.

"Alfred, my man, I have a task for you," Samson Strange said in serious tones.

"Is that so, guvnor? Wot sort of task might that be?"

"I want you to enter a cottage with a number of children in it and steal a conjurer's wand," said the Shapeshifter.

"And wot am I supposed to do with these 'ere kidlings while I carry out your design?" Alfred wondered.

"I don't know," growled the Shapeshifter. "You're the burglar. Use your initiative."

"And when would you want this act of purloinery carried out?" Alfred wondered.

"Today," said the Shapeshifter.

"Today!" exclaimed Alfred. "Mr Strange, I has a busy schedule. The best I can do is to fit you in in a week's time."

The Shapeshifter offered to pay him a sum of money that would be an adequate pension for the chairman of a bank. Alfred suddenly realised he had the time to do it, or, as he put it, a window in his diary.

The Shapeshifter gave him directions for Padhurst. Alfred wrote them down and clambered into his car, in which he rumbled into the distance.

But at the cottage in Padhurst, things were none too happy. Caroline's phone rang. It was her mother.

Darlene Zuppinger had received a call at the conference she was attending. The call came from the Police. Her husband had been, not alone arrested, but charged with embezzlement. He had been charged so quickly that it was clearly an open and shut case. Her friend Mrs Schneider, who lived across the road from her, was at the conference too and accompanied her to the police station. Mrs Schneider was not unacquainted with police stations, for her twenty-something sons drove like raving maniacs and both had been arrested in the past. The awful truth of Mr Zuppinger's downfall was conveyed tactfully to Caroline. It had been bad enough learning that her father was in league with the Shapeshifter, but this turned her whole life over in her head.

Gavin and Thomas had never seen Caroline cry. A tough egg was Caroline. But this was too much. A tear ran down the side of her nose. Then another. Caroline did not howl. She just began to sob hopelessly.

When the call was over, she explained what had happened and the two boys rushed to her aid. Gavin was even seen to put an arm around her and cuddle her, while Thomas rushed to get her a cup of tea, which is the panacaea in England. They believe there, in other words, that it is the remedy for all ills. A big tear splashed into the cup of tea when it arrived.

Some time after, they prepared to go to Pulborough. They told Caroline she didn't have to, but she was determined to tag along. However, the best laid plans of mice and men gang oft a-gley. Their door was unlocked and opened. There stood Aunt Dinah.

Aunt Dinah had one of those faces which fell naturally into disapproving lines. She also had a nose that looked as though it had been constructed for smelling out trouble. She raised her head slightly and looked around. She could see no sign of damage at first. The portrait of her formidable Aunt Euphemia, wearing a pince-nez, was staring from the wall. Items of porcelain and other decorations were unbroken. Then she looked down and saw a pig sitting on a rug in the corner.

Rover the dog she had known about. Rover was a dog noted for his sedentary habits. A pig was a different matter.

Pigs, I should tell you, are perfectly capable of being house-trained, as indeed Moccos was. Pigs are also clean animals, if appropriately looked after, as Moccos was too. But we live in a society that is *Piggist*. It has a prejudice against pigs which is undeserved. Pigs, I might add, are intelligent animals and Moccos was especially so. But Aunt Dinah had what might be called the *traditional attitude* towards pigs. To her, pigs were carriers of filth, lethal bacteria, unlethal but unpleasant bacteria, evil odours and probably some kind of plague. They were very much animals that belonged in the great outdoors. With a cry of horror she exclaimed, "Is that a *pig* over there?"

Of course, it could not be denied. Moreover, Moccos detected the hostility in Aunt Dinah's tone, and responded with a grunt which even the most dedicated pig lover could not deny was hostile.

"We didn't see it," said Gavin. "It must have come in through the other door. Thomas take it out."

So poor Moccos was removed from the premises and lay down in what may appropriately described as a disgruntled fashion on the grass outside.

Aunt Dinah's suspicions were now aroused. If this family had let a pig into her cottage, goodness knows what other deeds unmentionable it had wrought. She began to go around, gazing at the wallpaper for signs of drawings or graffiti, looking at her crystal vase to see if it was cracked, inspecting the carpet to see how urgent the need for hoovering was and in general holding the children's progress up no end.

She looked at the portrait of Aunt Euphemia disapprovingly, as though asking why the portrait of a dour Scotswoman had not prevented the desecration of her cottage by the swinish intruder.

Euphemia is a not uncommon Scottish name, as it is used in Scotland to anglicise the Gaelic name *Oighrig*. (I thought you might like to know that, though it has nothing to with the story).

Just then there was a knock at the door. Before Gavin could answer it, Aunt Dinah sailed over to it. She opened it to reveal the cheery features of Alfred the Yeggman.

"Morning, Missus," he said in what he deemed to be a cheeky Cockney voice. "Meter reader."

"The meter is over there, in the cupboard behind the kitchen door," said Aunt Dinah, indicating.

With a smile on his face Alfred entered the kitchen. Thomas, who was interested in everything, followed.

"What's your name?" he demanded, straying to the borderlands of impoliteness.

"Alfred," said Alfred.

"We named our fireplace Alfred," Thomas informed him.

"Why?" said Alfred, in genuine puzzlement.

"Because it's Alfred the Grate," supplied Thomas and he scampered into the other room.

Alfred returned in a few minutes.

"I've been looking at your meter," he said. "There's summat wrong with your lectrics. I'll have to examine the 'ouse."

"Are you a qualified electrician?" asked Aunt Dinah doubtfully.

" 'Course I am. I'll have to pull out all drawers, cupboards and receptacles to examine the walls behind them."

"And what exactly do you believe is wrong?" Aunt Dinah demanded.

"Well, I found the hyponautica must be detached somewhere from the monopode and there may be a defective argozotic," he informed her.

Aunt Dinah said nothing, but raised her stick and gave Alfred the Yeggman an almighty clout on the side of the head. He tumbled to the ground. She did not see him press a button on a device on his wrist.

"Imposter!" she proclaimed. "I have studied electronics myself and you are talking gibberish. You must be a burglar, trying to steal the family riches as you pretend to search the house for loose wires. I must hit you with my stick again. You seem insufficiently subdued."

And she did.

At that moment there was a thunderous knock on the door, which Gavin answered. A man in police uniform stood without.

"Sorry to disturb you," he said. "We've had a report of a burglar in the area and we're checking all the houses."

"You are just in time, Officer," declared Aunt Dinah. "This intruder is the man you were looking for."

The policeman strode over and seized Alfred.

"Now, now, come quietly, sir. I am arresting you on suspicion of housebreaking."

He went on to caution the dazed Alfred.

When they were outside, the burglar said, "Well done, Joe. I thought that old bag was goin' to murder me. That's the last time I do anything for Samson Strange." (In case you haven't twigged, the button he pressed on his wristband had summoned Joe).

"No trouble at all, boss," said Joe cheerfully.

Meanwhile, Aunt Dinah had decided the children could not be left on their own in case the experience had given them Post Traumatic Stress Disorder. The best remedy for this, she felt, was to set them a series of household tasks to keep their minds off the upsetting happening of the attempted larceny. This more or less put the kibosh on their going to Pulborough for the rest of the day.

Mother and Father returned at the usual time. Father had a rather delicate subject to broach with Mother and he felt now was as good a time as any. He explained what had happened to the Zuppingers and said Darlene had asked them to keep Caroline for a few more days.

Mother sent the children from the room. "I suppose it's all right," she said slowly, "but I don't relish the idea of having - well - a criminal's child under the same roof with *my* children."

This was the response Father had been fearing. This was why he had not raised the matter on the drive home from Horsham station.

"But we've known Caroline for years," he expostulated.

"That is not the point," said Mother sharply. "Caroline's status has changed now that her father has shown his criminal side."

Surprisingly, an outburst came from Aunt Dinah.

"Catherine, I am surprised at you," she proclaimed. "There is not one of us who does not have *some* ancestor who was a criminal. It's a statistical fact. Yet you have the temerity to look down your nose at this unfortunate child, who has done nothing wrong herself. You make me ashamed to be your aunt."

And, so saying, she strode out of the cottage.

****

We left Merlin the magician roaring mad and uttering strange utterances. He was hiding out in a clump of trees and living on berries (he knew, even in his madness, which ones were safe to eat) and then, on the same day of Aunt Dinah's dramatic visit, he went to a stream nearby. He saw his face in the water and the madness in his eyes and the shock of this drove the madness from him. He stood up and looked around warily. He saw Ganieda, his beauteous twin sister, approaching.

"So, Myrddin," she said, addressing him by his native name, "I see you are hale once more. Come, then, to my bower in the woodlands, where you may recover from your ordeal."

"Is it you, Gwendydd?" Merlin asked. "I thought myself back in the old days, when Rhydderch's men pursued me through bush and briar."

"Those days are long gone when you traversed the forests of Caledon, my brother," Ganieda responded. "Come with me."

****

That evening Gustavus arrived at the secret village of Logres.

"I have the Wand!" he called out joyfully on his approach.

Unfortunately, a Goblin, nearby and concealed, heard this and made his way to Margas, chief of the local Goblins. The latter tied a message to the leg of a sheerbird. The sheerbird is not a bird you will find in any book on bird watching. So swiftly does it fly, it has never been seen by the eye of man. To the house of the Shapeshifter it sped.

He now knew where Katy and the Wand were. He had now only to get Katy and bring them to the Rock of Gastry, where he would perform the ritual to bring the dreaded Demogorgon back to earth.

Chapter Thirty-four

The Reverend Ben Jarvis, B.A., B.D., was off to an important meeting next morning. He was meeting the Archpriest of Haccombe, about clerical matters which need not concern us here. He bade Katy farewell and climbed into his modest vehicle, unaware that from the bushes crafty Goblin eyes observed him. He drove out of the front gate and the Goblins emerged from the bushes.

The head of the Goblin group knocked upon the door. Katy, who was washing up the breakfast dishes, felt like swearing and would have done so, had it not been unbecoming for a Vicar's wife to swear. She couldn't abide interruptions, you see. She dried her hands and made for the door and half a dozen Goblins jumped in, grabbing her. Katy, however, was quite a hefty girl and fought back. She kicked one of the Goblins flying back out through the door, where he bumped into Mr Peabody, the verger, who had called to deliver a message. Unlike Katy, Mr Peabody was of frail construction and fell backwards, hitting his head. At length the Goblins overcame Katy and tied her up. If only Katy had had a dog, the struggle might have ended differently. But Katy had only a goldfish named Montmorency and goldfish are not noted for driving off intruders. Carrying her, they made off into the distance.

Mr Peabody had been knocked out for a couple of seconds and when he came to, he was somewhat dazed. Happily, old Mrs Pringle of the Ladies' Sewing Circle happened to be passing the gate.

"Mr Peabody, are you all right?" she asked.

Mr Peabody clearly was not. He staggered to his feet and said, "I think Mrs Jarvis has been kidnapped by youths in Hallowe'en costumes."

"We must call the Police at once," barked Mrs Pringle.

She whipped out her mobile. Soon a police car arrived upon the scene. There emerged from it two officers, one male and one female. The West Sussex Police Force was on the job.

Meanwhile, at the cottage in Padhurst, it had been a slightly awkward breakfast, as it had been a slightly awkward supper the night before. Everyone was trying not to mention such things as *prisons, crooks, criminals, lawbreakers* and the like, so the conversation had been strained, except in the case of Father who, in the absence of the *Daily Reporter* was reading a book called *Butterflies and Moths of the South Downs,* a volume into which he kept his nose firmly stuck. Even when Thomas knocked over the milk jug, Mother only uttered a staccato reprimand rather than the long spiel to which she would have given tongue on any similar occasion.

At length the parents departed. Gavin stood up. He had been told by Ganieda that he was a hero and this had given him the confidence to play the part of leader. He started issuing commands, telling his underlings to wear tracksuits and to equip themselves with any weapon that could be readily concealed. Who knew what might befall them that day? To their surprise, Caroline and Thomas found themselves carrying out his instructions. Before, they would have quibbled over this, argued over that. Not now. Gavin was definitely in charge.

He wondered if he should take the Terrible Weapon in the leather bag which Ganieda had given him. This would be a very dangerous thing to carry round, but he decided they might not be able to make it back before he needed to use it. They wondered about taking Moccos, but Caroline pointed out that they might not let him in the bus. Moccos showed no desire to go into the cottage. He seemed to have struck up a social relationship with a goat that was grazing on the grass behind the house.

They trooped to the nearest bus stop. It seemed several people were waiting for the Pulborough bus. There was an old man with a pipe, an old woman without a pipe and a woman who had the gleam of one who intends to go shopping in her eyes. There were a couple of others, whom I can only describe as nondescript.

The driver was a cheery soul, who greeted them as though he were taking them on a holiday. The bus sped smoothly into the distance.

By the time the children reached Pulborough, I am afraid Katy had been well and truly kidnapped. This did not mean the Vicarage was deserted, however. While the police had left, a gaggle of interested onlookers had gathered around the front gate. They were asking a rather shaken Mr Peabody for details of the Outrage. Mr Peabody was looking very much as though he would like them all to leave so he could go home, but he was far too much a gentleman of the old school to tell them so. The words, "Buzz off!" were foreign to his vocabulary. However, Mrs Pringle had taken on the part of his PA and spokesperson and she was regaling everyone with details of the event. Her not having seen it herself did not prevent her from unfolding the whole saga.

"They were teenagers dressed up like Robin Hood's Merry Men," she informed them, "but they were wearing masks, hideous they were. I reckon they came from up Oldcastle way, for we don't have folks like that in Pulborough, not that some of the youngsters don't get out of hand some times, but they never do anything like this."

"If they came from Oldcastle, they must have come in a car," one of the listeners pointed out.

"Of course they came in a car," Mrs Pringle concurred. "Mr Peabody agrees with me, don't you Mr Peabody? And Mrs Grimes said there was a strange car outside the Post Office this morning and-----" she lowered her voice as though about to reveal some ghastly secret-----"*it had a foreign number plate on it.*"

This caused an intake of breath. Mysterious foreigners. Probably spies. Not surprising with all these computers about. You could send messages everywhere.

"I always said that poor Mrs Jarvis was such a nice woman. But I sometimes felt she was a little - you know - rough at the edges," said a woman who felt herself to be Somebody.

"Don't speak ill of the dead," said a sombre man in a flat cap with wrinkles. I mean, he had wrinkles, the flat cap didn't.

"Dead!" cried a slightly deaf octogenarian. "Is she dead?"

"For all we know she is," said Flat Cap. "She may be starting to decompose in some field even as we speak."

Several of the women let out cries of horror. At this stage Mrs Pringle noticed that Mr Peabody had slipped away. Then a policeman came up and asked them to move along.

The children had turned up in time to hear most of this. They knew all too well from the description that it was not teenagers who had abducted Katy.

"Didn't Dr Vilnius say they were going to do the sacrifice at the Hill of Gastry," said Gavin. "We'll have to find out where it is and then head for it."

"Hold on," said Caroline. "They won't perform the sacrifice until they have the Wand. Gavin, weren't you told you had to use your Terrible Weapon to defend the Wand. They'll probably try to get it from Logres, now they have Katy. Gavin, you will need to get to Logres. Fine. Go there and Thomas and I will find this Ghastly Hill or whatever it's called."

Meanwhile, in the house of Samson Strange, the Shapeshifter had once again brought in Lilith from her distant location.

"We have the wench," he said sombrely. "The Wand is in Logres. There are but a handful of Dwarfs to defend it. Ready your forces, Lilith, and we will have the Wand this night."

Back in Pulborough, finding the Hill of Gastry had not proven too difficult a task. A local had informed them if they made their way to Coomberstown and turned left they would find it, a natural but isolated hill, in a field that belonged to a Mr Sourdough. They thanked him, then rang the Professor to tell him where they were.

The Professor was in buoyant mood. He was out of hospital. "Whatever you had," the Doctor had said, "you don't seem to have it now."

"I am home," the Prof informed them. "I can summon up help for you. Gavin, you go to the Hill of Gastry with the others. I'll send help to you to get you to Logres quickly. If the sacrifice is imminent, they must be intending to attack Logres soon and obtain the Wand. Another member of the Council of Wizards, Udaun the Leprechaun, has returned. He will help the rest of you stop the sacrifice."

So they made their way to Mr Sourdough's field, which was not difficult to find. They saw a small hill someway to their left. This must be the Hill of Gastry. In a corner of the field was a dilapidated building made of wood. It had clearly once served as a kind of sports pavilion, as it was built along the lines of such a structure, but the paint was peeling, the glass in the window was missing and there was every sign that it had not been used in a long time.

"Are you working for Professor Vilnius?"

The voice from behind startled them. They turned around to find a small man, about four feet tall, in bright clothing with fair hair facing them.

"Yes," said Caroline slowly, sizing up this unexpected apparition.

"I have come to guide one Gavin through the space tunnel. There is one not far from here. And he must bring with him the Terrible Weapon."

As none of the enemy knew about the Terrible Weapon, the three children realised this was no enemy feigning friendship. Gavin departed from the field with the elf (for such he was).

"Well, I suppose we'd better wait in the pavilion, so we see them before they see us," Caroline muttered. "I don't know what we can do to stop the sacrifice if they start to do it."

"I'm hungry," complained Thomas, who was hungry.

"Lucky I made sandwiches before we left, then," said Caroline, producing a packet from her shoulder bag.

The two began to scoff the sandwiches. They talked in uncouth fashion, with their mouths full, wondering what they would do if the Shapeshifter and his Goblins turned up. Thomas was sure help was on the way. Caroline was not so sure. Then they heard noises outside.

Very carefully they got down on their knees, then raised their heads so that they could see through the glassless window. Two men in long capes with hoods came first. Then came Goblins carrying Katy on a stretcher. She had clearly been drugged, she was quite unconscious. Finally came a troop of Goblins marching two by two, carrying spears. Their faces were misshapen and hideous. The two cloaked men and the Goblins with the stretcher went up the side of the hill until they reached the summit. The other Goblins formed a circle around the base.

"They're going to sacrifice her up there," breathed Thomas. "There's not a thing we can do."

At that moment they heard a thumping sound. It took them a couple of minutes to realise it was the sound of a horse's hooves on the grass. Then they saw it, a rather impressive horse and, on its back a small man in a green jacket and red trousers. He carried a spear, but it was no common spear. It seemed far too long for the little man who held it, yet her raised it up above his head. Its shaft was thick and its head too was thick, unlike the heads of most spears, yet it tapered to a point. Steam came from the head of the spear, which apparently had a small opening at the point, as though it were boiling, and gobbets of blood fell from the place where the spearhead joined the shaft and fell in thick semi-solid lumps onto the grass.

One of the men on top of the hill spoke.

"Who are you and what errand brings you hither, little man?"

The rider replied, "Udaun the Leprechaun they call me, the terror of the Western World. Behold, unless you set at liberty your captive, your doom is at hand. I carry here the Gae Bolga, the Lightning Spear, the most feared weapon used in days agone by Setanta the Tracker. Its sharpness is without equal and fiercer than its sharpness is its magic and fiercer than its magic is the destruction it wreaks. Behold, I have spoken."

Said the man on the hill, "We fear not tiny men such as thee, O little one. Go hence and hunt rats and mice and such small deer with your weapon, for they are of a meet size for you to combat. We scorn your threats and scoff at your fulminations. Blood will flow this day."

Said the Leprechaun, "Blood will flow indeed, but not your victim's. Behold the strength of the Gae Bolga."

And he flung the huge spear towards the hill and as he did so a peal of thunder rent the air and it landed amongst the Goblins. And a great crevasse opened at their feet and every one of them tumbled into it, with cries of woe and horror. And the ground closed over them and they were seen no more.

Then the Leprechaun drew forth his knife and cried, "Behold the Scian Uathbhasach, which in Sax-Bhearla means the Knife Abominable."

And from the point of the knife there came a beam of green light which split into two and each of the cloaked men was struck and they burst into flame and in but a moment were turned to ashes.

The Leprechaun wheeled his mount about and called out, "Young ones, come forth, for I know you are hidden nearby."

Slowly and carefully Caroline and Thomas, awed by the Leprechaun's power, quitted the pavilion. Thomas, however, continued to eat his sandwich, as he wasn't overawed enough to cease doing that. It was marmite, after all.

"Take the damsel to her home," he instructed them.

"She will be too heavy to carry," said Caroline doubtfully.

"What is that I see yonder in the field? It is a wheelbarrow. Place you the damsel in that and take her from this place."

They took the wheelbarrow up the hill and rather unceremoniously dumped poor Katy in it. Then they wheeled her back to the Vicarage.

Chapter Thirty-five

When Gavin and the Elf, whose name was Gylfi, emerged from the tunnel of space, they saw they were just outside the small hidden settlement of Logres. The log wall was manned by several Dwarfs armed with bows. There was a wooden shelf along the side of the wall, near the top of it, where they stood. They approached the gate in the wooden wall, which was opened for them and in they came, Gavin clutching the bag of leather which held the Terrible Weapon.

They went at once to the King's house. King Lamorak was within.

"Thrice welcome are you indeed," said the King, "for, even as we speak, Lilith and her army fare towards us through the forest. Go onto the parapet, so you may use the Terrible Weapon."

As Gavin crossed the way leading to the wall, he saw coming towards him a young man in warrior's gear whom he vaguely recognised. He would have placed him in his early twenties.

"Gavin!" cried this person. "Don't you recognise me?"

Gavin stared at the young man and then his jaw dropped.

"Yes, it's me, Gustavus, they've restored me to my proper age," cried the young warrior. "I am now twenty-two and I've managed to skip the difficult years of adolescence. Have you got" (he lowered his voice) "the Terrible Weapon?"

Gavin, still rather shocked by Gustavus Wilkins' sudden promotion to adulthood, nodded dumbly.

"Then come up to the parapet, for the enemy are coming through the forest."

Indeed, as Gavin mounted the parapet and gazed over the log wall, the first of Lilith's army of hags came into sight. To Gavin, who noticed that his fellow defenders were six dwarfs, two gnomes and Gyfi the elf, together with Gustavus, the enemy seemed a great throng. But it was not alone their number, but their aspect which seemed intimidating.

These crones looked as if they were decaying with age. Their arms looked thin, more like sticks than limbs. They carried spears tipped with stone that they looked too weak to hold. Their faces were wrinkled and raddled, as though bits of them might fall off at any moment. Their eyes were dull, with no spark of liveliness in them and their expressions were miserable, as though each harboured a secret sorrow. Their chins were bewhiskered and their hands had skin that was gnarled like the bark of a tree, but both their faces and hands were of a grey, unhealthy hue. They had no armour, but ragged garments, wispy and thin, about their persons. They were a host of withered women. As the advanced they took feeble steps, each time covering but a short space. They did not march, there was neither fife nor drum. But as they advanced they uttered a noise - I will not call it a tune or song - it was a kind of a low moan, each uttering it separately and not trying to keep in harmony with the others.

"They don't look up to much," observed Gavin. "Maybe we don't need the Terrible Weapon after all."

"They may look unnourished and frail," said Gylfi the Elf, "but each one of them has the strength of ten men."

As if to prove his point, one of them flung her spear at the walls. It hit the wood with a fierce thunk! And the spearhead went right through the wall, coming out at the other side.

The hags quitted the trees and advanced across the greensward before Logres. Gavin knew that it was time to bring the Terrible Weapon into play.

He thrust his hand into the bag and his fingers found what felt like thick hairs, which he gripped. He drew up from the bag a head, a large head, but neither he nor his fellow defenders looked at the face. But when the hags saw the face they stopped, in the fashion of a motion picture which is suddenly frozen. They were stilled, utterly, unable to move, and a dreadful change came over each of them. For, starting at their heads and going downwards, they proceeded to turn into stone. It was as though a painter applied his brush to canvas and swept it downwards, they turned to stone first at their heads and then down went the change to the soles of their feet, this lasting only a few seconds. There they stood, an army of stone. But the stone did not look like solid rock, stout and resistant, but rather like the crumbling stone of rocks that might disintegrate at any moment. Even as Gavin looked on, the odd crumb of stone fell from one of the hideous statues he had created. The hags were a threat no longer, for the Terrible Weapon was the head of Medusa the Gorgon, which changed all who gazed on it into stone. Seeing the enemy was overcome, Gavin pushed the head back into the bag, swiftly as possible, and noted with some repugnance that, instead of hair, there were dead serpents on top of it and it was by these he was holding them.

But then Lilith herself strode to the fore from the trees. She was impervious to the head, she was too powerful for it to wreak its magic on her. She was a tall woman, fair of hair, dressed in light armour and carrying in her right hand a sword.

And she called out, "Come forth, Lamorak, King of Logres. By magic you have slaughtered my army, not by the doughty deeds of warriors. Well, then, face me in single combat, each against the other without help, or be accounted a coward amongst warriors."

From the parapet, King Lamorak replied, "Do you think I fear you, Lilith who dwells by the sea? Ready yourself, for never was it said that Lamorak of Logres refused a challenge."

So King Lamorak ordered the gates to be thrown open and strode forth, carrying a sword longer and more deadly than that of Lilith. And the two faced each other on the sward and the face of Lamorak was as fierce as that of Hector the horse-tamer, but that of Lilith was more calculating, assessing her opponent.

And the two came together and Lamorak struck a mighty blow which Lilith parried and surprised the King with the strength wherewith she parried it., for Lilith had the strength of two score warriors. Now the left hand of Lilith was behind her back, Lamorak thinking she had placed it there so he would not cut it off in the swordplay. But it held a dagger, of the type called by the French a *main-a-gauche*, and, as she struggled to hold off Lamorak's sword, she whipped this around and plunged it into his vitals. And Lamorak doubled up with pain and leaned forward and, with one blow, Lilith struck the head from his body, so that it landed on the grass.

Lilith gazed defiantly up at the parapet, whence all looked on in horror. Then she vanished, going whither I know not.

And Lamorak of the House of Arthur was dead.

Chapter Thirty-six

The sight of two children (Caroline and Thomas) wheeling a wheelbarrow containing an unconscious vicar's wife along the footpaths of Pulborough could not but attract attention. Some thought Katy in the wheelbarrow might be dead until they heard her snoring slightly, which dispelled that impression. Most of those who saw this spectacle thought they should do something, but weren't quite sure *what*. Several people began to follow them, much to the children's discomfort. At length they reached the Vicarage.

The Reverend Ben Jarvis on perceiving his unconscious wife coming up the garden path rushed from his doorway.

"I think she's been drugged," said Caroline.

"We found her in a field," said Thomas, wisely saying nothing much else. He knew no one would believe the story of Katy's rescue by a Leprechaun on a horse.

A doctor was summoned. He said that Katy should be taken to hospital for observation. At that moment Katy revived.

Katy was one of those people who didn't like hospitals and said she was perfectly all right. Yes, she had been given a drug, but it had worn off now.

The doctor, a whit disgruntled, departed. Next to arrive were the police. Detective Sergeant Snodgrass wanted full details of her ordeal. Who had captured her? All she could say was they were nasty looking men with red caps. They had given her some kind of draught and she remembered no more.

The children's claim that they had found her unconscious in a field was not questioned.

"Maybe we better go back to Padhurst now and wait for Gavin to return," Caroline suggested.

The Vicar persuaded his curate to drive them. The Vicar would have done it himself, only he had to look after Katy.

The distance by road from Pulborough, through the twisting lanes of Sussex, was not long by car. They found Rover waiting anxiously for them inside the cottage and Moccos there too, with his master, Merlin, who had recovered his recently lost wits. Rover wasn't too sure about Merlin and had been looking on him with a mistrustful eye.

Merlin - by what means I do not know - had been informed of Gavin's victory and the tragic death of King Lamorak.

"Gavin wiped out a monstrous army," said Thomas. "Cool. Wish I'd been there."

"Who will be the new king?" asked Caroline, remembering King Lamorak hadn't been married with children.

"It will be Gustavus Wilkins," said Merlin. "Although he doesn't know it, he's Lamorak's cousin. When he was little he was kidnapped and dumped in that awful orphanage."

"What about the bride - the princess of the hidden city in South America that they were bringing to King Lamorak?" wondered Caroline.

"She's only seventeen," supplied Merlin, "so she can marry Gustavus instead."

"That's handy," opined Thomas. "It just shows you never know who you'll end up married to."

He cast a sidelong glance at Caroline, which she didn't notice.

That evening Gavin arrived home - Gylfi the Elf had escorted him through the tunnel of distance again. He looked rather tired. They had told Gustavus he was to be the next King of Logres and the expression on his face had been somewhat comical, especially when they told him that he would be marrying an Inca princess in a couple of weeks.

"Being grown up will take some time to adjust to," said Merlin.

Gylfi the Elf departed just as they heard Father's car arriving on the drive. Both Father and Mother got out.

"I think I shall get out by the back window," said Merlin. "I don't really want your Mother to have a fit when she sees me. Come on, Moccos."

Meanwhile word had been brought to the Shapeshifter of the utter failure of his designs. First, he had been sent a message by the local Goblin chief of the failure of the sacrifice, the spectacular nature of which had been witnessed by a Goblin from afar. Then came word of the destruction of Lilith's forces. That evening he chafed. Going into his back garden, he thought,

"It is the Taylors of Hillford who have done this to me. And the Oracle says they will destroy me. I have tarried long enough. I must go and kill them."

This would mean making his way to Padhurst, but Padhurst was not far. He went into his back garden. All at once he began to change into the horrendous beast, which was these days known as the Beast of Petworth. Then he went charging across the fields, foam spraying from his ghastly mouth, stopping every few minutes to utter a howl. He charged towards the cottage, but this was strange. It looked deserted. There were no lights within, the flickering caused by a television was not to be seen, even though the curtains were undrawn. Then he heard voices.

Mother and Father were getting into the car, where the children already sat. The building operations in Hillford were complete. The Taylors were going back home. The Shapeshifter heard car doors slam and the car started off.

Frustration tore through the Beast. He uttered a loud howl.

"What was that?" wondered Father.

"It sounded like a loud howl," supplied Thomas.

"Probably a vixen," said Caroline, who knew about nature. "They can sound pretty eerie."

As the car moved through the encroaching shadows, Mother, looking in the rearview mirror, muttered, "Harold, there's some kind of animal chasing the car."

The children in the back seat looked backwards. They had little doubt about what it was.

"Well, if it wants to attack us, it won't do us much harm," said Father, keeping his eyes on the road ahead. "It's not that pig that's been hanging around the cottage, is it?"

"I never saw a pig that could run that fast," said Mother.

Just at that moment a large truck approached from the opposite direction. The Beast hopped to one side to avoid it, jumping over a field gate.

"Well, whatever it was, we've left it behind," stated Father.

Ah, Father, you are wrong. Animals don't have to travel by road. The Beast is following you through the fields, o'erleaping hedges and scaring cows the while. He is headed for Hillford, intent on destroying the Taylors of Hillford ere they destroy him. Watch out, Father (and passengers).

The car pulled into the driveway at Hillford in due course. The Taylors little knew of a drama unfolding just outside the town. In a field nearby, Myrtle Singleton, this time with her camera at the ready, was hunting the Beast. The field also contained a cow named Dulcie, but she doesn't come into the story and, in the distance, our old friend Fanshaw spelled Featherstonehaugh. Then it contained something else. Over the bordering hedge jumped the Beast and it made straight for Myrtle. It charged and grabbed her head between its massive jaws, but, before it could close them in a sickening crunch, Fanshaw had grabbed it by the tail and given it a massive yank. Dropping Myrtle, the Beast turned around and that would have been the doom of Fanshaw had not a patrol of farmers with shotguns, trying to find the animal that had been preying on their cattle, entered the field. The Beast realised discretion was the better part of valour: it turned and fled and had jumped the next hedge before the farmers could open fire. Myrtle, who was somewhat shocked by having her head clamped between the Beast's jaws, looked adoringly at Fanshaw.

"You saved my life," she cried, throwing her arms around his neck in a staggering embrace and knocking him over, so that both fell into a cowpat, but somehow they didn't mind. It was the start of a Great Romance.

The farmers didn't catch up with the Beast as it had gone far ahead by the time they had helped the young couple to their feet. The Beast was still heading for Hillford, the lights of which twinkled in the distance. The Oracle had told him, he reasoned, that the Taylors would kill him, but that was a deed they could never accomplish if he killed them first. When he entered the town he kept to back lanes and snickets. Cats, rats and other denizens of the night fled at his approach. And then he was at the top of Hazel Road, where the Taylors lived.

Samson Strange, Shapeshifter and Beast, looked about him. He knew which house was the Taylors'. And there, outside it, was Father, putting out the bin.

Father was a bit disgruntled. The Schneider boys were driving around the place at speed in their car, apparently not going anywhere, but driving back and forth just for kicks. *I'm going to report those two to the Police,* he thought. *They're a blooming menace, even if I do know their parents.*

Then, looking up, he saw the Beast charging towards him with slavering jaws. Father did not linger. Though no athlete, as the Beast rushed towards him, Father began to display powers of speed he had never guessed he harboured. Then, at that very moment, the Schneiders in their vehicle entered the road and drove straight in his direction. Father leapt agilely to one side and the car hit the Beast with a mighty splat.

The screech of brakes, which the Schneiders had tried to put on too late, drew faces to windows, all along the road. The two young Schneiders emerged from the car.

"I think we've hit a dog," said one.

But when they went around to the car, there was no dog but the dead body of the Shapeshifter.

"It's a bloke," gasped one of the Schneiders in horror.

Gavin, Thomas and Caroline came out of their front door, followed by Mother. Although the light was fading, Gavin said, "Look - the Shapeshifter."

Mother gave a great cry, "It's Samson Strange!" Then she told the children to go inside, on the grounds that this sort of scene was far too traumatic for persons of their tender years to see. As she advanced, a sudden thought occurred to her, *I can write an article on this for the magazine. They'll pay me a bundle for it.*

Oh, Mother, what an unworthy thought. Unworthy, but understandable.

So perished Samson Strange, the Shapeshifter. All his plans to bring back Demogorgon had failed. In the small universe to which Demogorgon had been consigned, he was not wist of any of this.

The Police were called in, as was necessary, over the death, but the Schneiders were never prosecuted. The Police heard so many stories of a strange Beast, backed up by farmers from the nearby fields, that they decided what must have happened was that the Schneiders had swerved to avoid a dog and struck the Shapeshifter unintentionally. Happily, neither had been drinking and no charges were brought. However, the two young Schneiders had been badly shocked and subsequently purchased bicycles.

Darlene Zuppinger, after her husband's conviction, decided to stay on in England, as she had a good job there. When Caroline told Gavin this, Thomas felt his face showed that he was strangely pleased. A grin spread over Thomas's face. He knew what lay ahead.

The Order of Demogorgon started scheming again to find a way to release Demogorgon. To date, they haven't managed it.

The authorities closed down the Good Hope Orphanage. I would hope no similar institutions exist.

In the hidden settlement of Logres, King Gustavus was crowned and in that kingdom all was glam and glee. He had married the princess of Gran Paititi and the kingdom of Logres settled down into stability, the Goblins giving it a wide berth.

George Featherstonehaugh pronounced Fanshaw married Myrtle Singleton later that year. He has given up cryptozoology on the grounds of danger and taken up trainspotting.

Several days after the Shapeshifter's death, Alvis was to be found in his house. He had a black plastic bag into which he was putting everything of value he could lay his hands on, before anyone else turned up to claim it. He couldn't fit Samson's computer into his bag, but he reasoned that, as computers went out of date so quickly, it wasn't worth it.

Having plundered the ground floor, the made his way to the upper storey. While he was busily looting this, he heard footsteps downstairs. He descended cautiously. He didn't want to be attacked by another looter.

He found no looter, but Dr Petroc Vilnius. He had no idea who he was, but he didn't look as if he were there for evil purposes.

"Good afternoon," said Alvis. "I am Alvis, the late Samson Strange's butler. I'm just doing some tidying up."

I don't know if the Prof guessed what sort of tidying up he was doing, but he said, "So sad about your employer's death."

"There was one strange thing about it," said Alvis thoughtfully. "He had - I suppose you'd call it a premonition - that he would be killed by people named Taylor. He often had such premonitions, but he said they weren't premonitions, he said he could find out things about the future. The thing is, he was usually correct. But he was wrong this time. He wasn't killed by anyone named Taylor. He was run down by people named Schneider."

Dr Petroc Vilnius looked thoughtfully at Alvis. "Schneider is the German for Taylor," he informed him quietly.

Some time later, Gavin and Caroline had a quarrel. (They had one about every two months.)

"I'll never speak to you again!" stormed Gavin.

"Likewise," bellowed Caroline.

Thomas grinned. He knew better.